The

M.B.A.

How to Build a Business That You Love and Take Control of Your Finances Without Losing Who You Are

David Schloss

The New MBA

How to Build a Business That You Love and Take Control of Your Finances Without Losing Who You Are

ISBN: 978-0-578-64318-2 (paperback)

SHAMELESS BRIBE

I have a special gift for you to help you on your entrepreneurial journey.

Don't forget to get your resources, too! Grab them at http://thenewmbabook.com/freegift

TABLE OF CONTENTS

FOREWORD

Very few people that I've met come across as confident and humble. David has that quality. He doesn't push his experience on you. Like a wise vet of the game, he shows you the shortest path to your destination and urges you to take the next step.

Not too long ago, I watched a video by Prince EA about Millennials vs. Baby Boomers. It was a rap battle. At the beginning of the rap, he and the old man diss each other. About halfway through, Prince EA flips the script. He questions why every generation talks down on the next generation. He says Millennials have different life perspectives because of internet access. That doesn't make them lazy.

By the end of the five-minute clip, both sides agree that Millennials will be better off if previous generations help them grow instead of trash talking them.

Every generation needs to hear from members of its own generation about what it takes to be successful. It's one thing to hear it from the "old heads", like me. It's another thing to hear it from someone your own age.

The first time I met David, he was hanging out in the hotel lounge to meet with attendees at an event. He'd skipped through some of his slides during his presentation and wanted to make himself available afterwards. With a small group of listeners at his table, he broke down social media marketing principles like it was elementary math. And, he was just as excited off of the stage as he was on it.

David is a Millennial on a mission. He wants his generation to win. In my twenties, I only dreamed about making real money and traveling the world, talking to crowds about how they, too, could be successful. But, I was careless with my money. I spent it as soon as it came in. That's one thing that I found particularly useful in this book.

David doesn't just teach you how to make money in business, build long-term connections, and scale your profits. He gives you a strategy for how to handle your finances. He's imparting his experiences as a self-made entrepreneur, an accomplished businessman, and a budding investor to you. You are his people.

This book is a guide to helping Millennials carve out their own space in the entrepreneurial world. But, at the heart of it, there's a deeper message for you. That message is this: regardless of what the media says, you have everything you need to succeed in whatever industry you want to be in, and I can teach you how to do it in this age of the knowledge worker.

David does a brilliant job of showing you how to earn your New MBA in this new economy. And, with practice, patience, and persistence, you'll have Millennial Business Authority.

D Arlando Fortune

Founder, GFMandC, LLC

Author of "Unlimited Potential"

DEDICATION

This book is dedicated to everyone looking to turn their dream into reality. It takes practice, patience, and persistence to reach your goals.

Never give up.

INTRODUCTION

You've been deceived. The title is *The New MBA,* but it has little to do with formal education. MBA stands for Millennial Business Authority, but if you're not a Millennial, don't worry, the advice given in this book is suitable for anybody who wishes to start a new business. I would be delighted if any budding entrepreneur used the information in this book to start a business, be they 15 years old or 80.

The subtitle of the book tells you more, referring to how to "create, grow, and scale" your business, because I assume that, while you want to start a small business, you don't want it to stay small. If you want to set up a small business and keep it small, that's entirely your prerogative, and there's nothing wrong with that, but this book isn't just about what you need to know to set up a small business, it's also about growing business, scaling it, and making it highly successful and thriving.

I've focused on the Millennial generation for two reasons. One, I am a Millennial myself. Two, Millennials are facing a set of unique challenges; challenges their parents, grandparents, and even great-grandparents did not face.

The world has changed dramatically in the last 70 years and continues to change. Because of this, the Millennial generation could do with the insight I hope this book provides. Let's take a little look at what it means to be a Millennial and remove the deceptions that, at first glance, seem discouraging.

THE PLIGHT OF THE MILLENNIAL

What exactly is the Millennial generation? Though the term itself is a huge overgeneralization, it is a widely accepted definition a member of the Millennial generation was born between 1981 and 1996. If you're reading this book in the year of its publication, 2020, and you're between 23 and 38 years of age, you fit this definition. Please don't get too hung up if you're a few years older (Gen X) or younger (Gen Z).

This is an important distinction because it's critical to understanding the challenges faced by Millennials (and, for that matter, post-Millennials) and how the environment differs, especially from a business perspective, to that faced by Baby Boomers and Generation Xers.

Baby Boomers came into a world that had begun to shuck off the human and financial costs of the Second World War (1939-45). The population was on the rise. So was the economy. The notion of a job for life was very real, and many people took advantage of this by staying in the same role with the same company their whole lives. In a booming economy, there were also opportunities for entrepreneurs, and many businesses that are household names today were born in this era. If you follow the growth of big businesses in the last 50 years, you'll see companies that serve Baby Boomers explode. *

Generation X continued to enjoy these fruits, possibly even more so, as the economy continued to flourish. But things were beginning to change. Without going into a massive history lesson, let's look at some of the biggest challenges facing the Millennial generation.

By the way, this isn't a whine (as other generations claim we do incessantly). This is a hard-nosed look at the different, harsher business environment in which we live today. Strategies for starting a business must adapt to the new world, and although things are tougher nowadays than they were, there are still thousands of different opportunities. Let's look at the world of the Millennial.

High unemployment rates. Almost 40% of our nation's unemployed are Millennials.

Devalued nature of education. Millennials are, to date, the most educated generation ever. Over 60% have gone to college. This sounds great (to set up a business, it is great, for reasons we'll come on to later), but problems arise when you realize the number of jobs requiring degrees is lower than the number of people with degrees.

This is one of the reasons nearly 40% of the workforce* under-25 either don't have enough work or are completely unemployed. The Millennials who have been lucky enough to get a job have found it increasingly difficult to get one that matches their degree qualifications. Only 55% of Millennials got jobs that were relevant to their study areas.

High student debt. The cost of student debt has mushroomed* in the last decade. Current figures indicate students, or former students, owe nearly 1.5 trillion dollars in student loans, three times higher than it was a decade ago, and was a record back then. Also, student debt is unique in that, even if you're declared bankrupt in later life, it never goes away until it's paid. Over 40% of Millennials are saddled with this debt, and many of them currently can't pay it. (More on student debt and how to handle it in Chapter 7.)

Average earnings have plummeted. In 2000, a young person (anybody primarily in their twenties) was earning an average of approximately $37,000 a year. In 2019, this fell to as low as $32,000 a year.

Homeownership is out of reach for many Millennials. More and more Millennials are living at home than in previous generations, mainly because fewer of them can afford to be homeowners.*

Fewer Millennials are financially sound. A recent Washington Post survey provided instant insight into just how precarious the financial lives of Millennials were. 63% of Millennials would struggle to cover an unexpected expense of $500 or more. Only 6% of Millennials feel they're making a lot more than required to cover basic needs. 44% of them said, were they to win the lottery, $5,000 of it would immediately go to paying off outstanding loans and bills, which implies a severe difficulty in being able to save or invest money.

Stress, depression, and anxiety. With such limited financial opportunities, it's hardly surprising Millennials are harder hit by depression and stress than previous generations. 75% of Millennials have suffered from on-the-job depression, compared to approximately 50% of Gen Xers and Baby Boomers. Depression is shown to be on the decline for most Americans – except for the Millennial generation.

Fewer Millennials own their own businesses. A report from the Catchment Foundation indicates Millennials made up approximately 23% of new entrepreneurs in the year 2013. In 1996, the ratio of new entrepreneurs between 16 and 32 years of age was 35%. Based on the stats, business ownership should be going up, not down.

Millennials get bad press. Type in the word "Millennial" in Google, and you will find a slew of negative stereotypes. Millennials are entitled. Millennials need constant reassurance and approval for everything. Millennials are praise-hungry and over-sensitive. Millennials are obsessed with technology and over-distracted by it. Millennials change jobs more frequently than many people change their suits. Millennials expect special privileges from their jobs. And, to bring them all together in one moniker, Millennials are Generation Snowflake. (Really?!)

Almost every one of the criticisms above is lazy and inaccurate, little more than journalistic horse manure. (I'm a father now so no potty language.) Since the Second World War, and probably before, it seems almost a requirement for one generation to disparage and criticize the generation after it. The Millennial generation has suffered greatly for this because we are currently amid some of the most profound changes to our society. Yes, there have been several technological advances in previous generations but none so drastic, frequent, or revolutionary, as seen in our generation.

Take the accusation Millennials are job-hoppers. A big factor in this is the fact there are no longer as many secure jobs available, and there are more jobs that use zero-hours contracts. This means the nature* of available jobs has become more inherently insecure, unstable, and short-term. The belief Millennials are job-hoppers takes none of this into consideration.

YOU'RE IN CONTROL

I hope you're still with me and not too depressed. I felt it was necessary to dive into the details of how dire our circumstances appear before showing you the opportunity hidden within it. I promise you it is not as bad as it sounds. What hasn't changed is the fact you're in control of how you respond to this new environment. You're still the master of your own fate.

There's an exercise improv teams play called the "Yes/No" game. In this game, a partner would play a scene where they describe something disastrous that has happened to them. For example, a partner might say, "My wife left me, and I am all alone." You might say something like, "Yes, and they do a fantastic range of meals for one of my local stores. And I can take full advantage of them."

My point is this. Many of the new situations unique to Millennials can be converted into positives. The way you view something, either as a problem or as an opportunity, can profoundly alter your response to situations and be the difference between an uncertain future or one in which you're in control of your destiny. For example:

- Millennials have a 40% unemployment rate – yes, and this means 60% of them do have jobs. For those who don't have jobs, starting their own business might be the way to go.

- My degree doesn't mean as much as it used to – yes, which means I have an opportunity to exploit the intelligence, persistence, and hard work required in getting my degree to starting my own business. Heck, I could even start a business based on my degree!

- I have high student debt, have low average earnings, and I'm in a financially precarious position – yes, and this means starting my own business with a low start-up cost could potentially be an ideal way to bump my average earnings up, get rid of some of the high student debt, and put myself on a firm financial footing.

- Fewer and fewer Millennials own their own businesses – yes, which means you will have an opportunity to stand out from the crowd more easily.

- Millennials get a bad press – yes. Actually, yes and nothing. Let lazy journalists and TV anchors spout irrelevant nonsense if it makes them feel better. What should it mean to you? Exactly. Nothing.

Even with the newer challenges facing Millennials, there are still bucket loads of opportunities out there, and there are some pretty great things about being a Millennial, too.

ADVANTAGES OF BEING A MILLENNIAL

First and foremost, it's all about technology. It is hard to overestimate the profound difference technology has made to our lives.

Consider the life of a Gen Xer, born in the mid-1970s, compared to a Millennial born in the mid-1990s. Just 20 years difference. At the age of 22, our Gen Xer would possibly have heard of the internet, but probably not had access to it, unless they were extremely lucky, or a member of the military.

By the age of 22, in 2007, our Millennial probably would not have known a life without some access (possibly loads) to the Internet. Two of the currently most visited sites in the world, Facebook and YouTube, were created in 2004 and 2005, respectively, and both gained massive traction almost immediately. Many Millennials may not even remember a time before Facebook.

Mobile phones and smartphones. Our 22-year-old Gen Xer may have seen mobile phones in action, may even have had one, although pagers were more of a thing in the 90s. But the phones of those days would certainly have been primitive compared to nowadays. They certainly wouldn't have provided internet access.

By contrast, our Millennial would have probably owned a mobile phone, which they could use to communicate via text or

24

voice, send and receive emails, buy almost anything, surf social media, and access almost any website anywhere in the world. The smart technology behind these phones gave birth to the tablet, and similar smart devices, untying people from their home computers and landlocked telephones.

If our 22-year-old Gen Xer were joining the workforce, they would have seen the massive computers with a huge base sat at the feet of workers going through its death throes. The technology available to our Millennial was about to make working from anywhere, not just a possibility, but a reality.

The Internet. One of the biggest differences between Millennials and any other generation is their unprecedented access to billions of people via the internet. This is not an exaggeration. There are 7.25 billion people in the world, and most recent figures indicate that over 3 billion of them have access to the internet in one way or another. Millennials enjoy access to more people. Therefore, the quality of information available has also skyrocketed. This access is a huge advantage for you as you start your business.

This is only a shortlist of advantages that support starting your own business. There are many more outside of this list. (They're only a web search away. Do that later.)

Constant change. Millennials have lived through some of the most astonishing changes to society thus far. Not all these changes have been good either; for instance, the effects of climate change. Living in a state of constant change has given Millennials the advantage of being able to adapt to flexible working patterns and change things up when required. This is a valuable skill for a budding entrepreneur because things are bound to change when you least expect it, and you must be able to adapt.

Better education. I've already highlighted the higher education standard of Millennials, and in terms of starting a business, it gives them a head start. It doesn't necessarily mean Millennials can start a business based on their degrees. It means they have demonstrated a measure of critical reasoning, analysis, creative writing, and a whole bundle of other skills that can transfer into starting up a successful business. Getting a degree takes hard work and persistence, which are essential entrepreneurial qualities.

That doesn't mean you won't succeed in business without a degree. There are plenty of examples of successful people who didn't complete formal education. Bill Gates, for one!

An entrepreneurial mindset. Because of the diversity and variety of jobs Millennials have been willing to go through to make ends meet, their ability to roll with the punches of our current economy and keep going are fantastic qualities for any budding entrepreneur.

It's a lovely word, entrepreneur. If you want to set up your own business or businesses, you're not an entrepreneur. You become one as soon as you make the decision to become one and take action to realize your dreams.

I should know. I was born and raised in Miami, Florida, and I've been in business since 2007, where I started from my college apartment. I am a serial entrepreneur, agency owner, investor, author, and speaker. And, of course, I am a Millennial!

THE FIVE STEPS UNVEILED

Hopefully, you see the deception. You do not have to be another statistic or gross generalization. It's time for you to create, grow, and scale a thriving business in the 21st century. These are the five steps to take:

1. **Get Started Right** speaks for itself. This will involve an approach to working out what you can do to generate income from your business as soon as possible and how to start without needing a pot of money in the first place.

2. **Use The Three Ps Of Longevity** provides the qualities you need to make sure your business is not just successful at the start but for a very long time.

3. **Find A Business That Suits Your Personality** is all about finding a business approach that suits your personality, particularly when it comes to selling.

4. **Forge Productive Relationships** will provide you with insight into forging productive relationships, without which most businesses will die on the vine.

5. **Master Financial Literacy** is a detailed look at all things financial and will look at how to create a sound financial base, how to help your business grow, and finally, what to do with your increasing profits long-term.

It's not expensive to start your first business and get yourself onto the foothills of entrepreneurship. I can personally attest to that. When you're willing to make an effort to clean out your negative beliefs and truly believe in yourself and your ability to start a business, you can make it.

It does require work. No escaping that. It also requires ensuring you get your finances in order so that you can move through your day and the rest of your life in a stress-free manner. Hard work, positive self-belief, and financial acumen are the true ingredients for success. Positive self-belief and financial acumen can be learned, like any skill, provided you put in the hard work.

This book offers you the knowledge and understanding of how to take your ideas, turn them into assets, start earning online, and how you can establish yourself as an authority.

How to Use This Book

1. Read this book all the way through. All sections are closely linked.

2. While reading, make as many notes as you can. Jot down your ideas, your questions, anything you think will help you set up and maintain successful businesses.

3. When you get to the end, start again, this time with your notes in front of you. You may find there are things you've missed the first time around.

While it will do you no harm to read this book as many times as you can manage, if you've read it twice, it's best to stop reading while you're getting started. Because now, it's time to just DO IT!

CHAPTER 1

Step 1 – Get Started Right

In this chapter, I'm going to talk about the quickest way to make money from your own talents and how to get started quickly. I'm going to provide you with a specific process for tapping into your own talents, experiences, and skillsets and monetizing them.

But, before we go into that, it's worthwhile taking a more holistic look at your life. Forget it being just about business. Forget it being about your family life or your spiritual journey. The single best thing you can do now is to pause and take a few hours to commit to a helicopter view of everything. When you go into business, you could end up doing something that will consume large parts of your days, weeks, and months. It's well worth doing this first.

TAKING A LIFE INVENTORY

This is your helicopter view. What I'm suggesting you do is take a cool, dispassionate look at where your life is and where you want it to be. I appreciate that for many this can be difficult, but I promise if you commit to at least some of these exercises and just give yourself an idea of what you want your life to be all about, you're much more likely to move into areas of business that are suitable to you, even you enjoy. With a wider view of your life and a plan for the future, you're much more likely to stick with it when the going gets tough.

For the Millennial working out what's best for him or her, one of the first questions they may ask is – should I start my own business? Or, should I look for one of those increasingly elusive stable jobs with regular pay? If I do start a new business, how do I learn how to do it, and where would I learn how to start? What resources would I need? How would I support myself financially if it starts slowly? Who else would support me, and not necessarily just financially, but emotionally too? Could I cope with the emotional and physical stress that comes with starting a new business?

These are the questions I asked myself. I went back and forth for quite some time with the idea of continuing my new business or finding a stable job. Like any new business, I had a lot of uncertainty in the first few years, and my family didn't support the idea at all. I know they wanted what was best for me, which for them was seeing me getting a steady job with a regular income, but deep down, I knew I would be just another depressing statistic in a regular job. The only person who supported me unequivocally was my girlfriend, and I'll never forget that. I am so happy that I followed my heart, my gut, my instinct, or whatever you want to call it.

If you're feeling any of these uncertainties, you know at some stage you're going to have to decide – stay where you are and be uncertain, unhappy, and possibly broke. Or give yourself a fighting chance at a better life, at a life that suits you. I presume by reading this book, you at least have a passing interest in starting your own business. Now is a good time to go through a life inventory. As you go through these exercises, write down your answers. If you have a friend who will lend you a neutral ear, talk through the exercises that give you the most trouble.

Consider the things you don't want

Asking yourself what you don't want is much more powerful than asking what you do want. It requires deeper thinking and indirectly covers what you DO want anyway. To ask what you don't want to do requires you to think about what makes you unhappy.

You may come up with several answers. For example, some of the examples below are my answers, and some are culled from other people, but they are all genuine answers. I have confined it to asking about the working environment. Some of the things people said they don't like include:

- Working with large crowds of people.
- Feeling trapped or stuck in a job.

- Making presentations.

- Working late.

- Working fixed hours.

- Working 9-5.

- Limited or zero chances of promotion.

- Dealing with members of the public.

- Working in a team.

- Working alone.

- Not having enough money.

You can see the variety. If you're doing this for yourself, you will spot patterns in your answers. For example, I don't like feeling trapped in a job, working fixed hours, or working in an environment where there are limited chances for advancement. I also want to make sure I am earning enough to pay all the bills at the end of each month and be able to save enough for what I call my survival fund and enough for those emergencies that occur once in a while – be they medical, mechanical, or anything else. We'll talk in much more detail about finances later in this book.

I want to avoid an environment where any of these are featured. You can identify the things you dislike the most and, when considering what you want to do with your life, think about how important avoiding them are. The main thing is to focus on the experiences you do want.

Make sure they are experiences that will contribute to your well-being. For example, I like the experience of learning new things. I like the experience of traveling and experiencing new places. And I like the company of my family and friends. Any vocational career I follow must include at least some of these for me to be fulfilled.

Find people you admire and/or envy

When we get into the business side of things, I'm going to talk about the advantages of finding mentors. For the purposes of this exercise, look at everybody around you. This doesn't have to be people you know directly, but if there are people in the world who you admire, or whose life you aspire to, consider why. Why do you admire or envy them? Is it because of what they do? Is it the impact they have on other people? How much they get paid? The size of their family? Or is it that all these factors appeal to you?

For example, take Jeff Bezos, founder and CEO of business Goliath, Amazon. (I don't want to get into the ins and outs of how Amazon runs because it's controversial). One admirable thing about Jeff Bezos is how he set up Amazon in 1993 from the back of his garage – initially as just an online bookstore – and did two things that have contributed to the phenomenal dominance Amazon enjoys.

First, he kept things simple. Every year, Amazon's mission statement is written on the equivalent of one side of an A4 piece of paper. Every year it changes to match the times. Second, he spent (and still spends) a lot of time looking into the future, predicting trends, and pointing Amazon in that direction. His simplicity and his ability to innovate and change his business with the business tide are things I admire about him.

You may not agree with my choice. The point is to pinpoint people who *you* admire and to work out why. By working out why you admire them, you're identifying what it is about yourself you want to see or want other people to see in you.

Think about the people who have been in your life over the years, the ones you admire. If they are still in your life, don't be afraid to talk to them, ask them how they do things, and ask them what their secrets are. Again, you'll find out new things about how to run businesses. You'll also find out more about yourself in this process. The people you admire or envy (as bad as that sounds) are great indicators of what you want from your life, whether consciously or subconsciously.

Think about the activities you love outside of work

Is it running, cycling, a good book, or a movie? There are two reasons to think about this. One is because you will want to make sure they form part of your lifestyle if you're setting up a new business. Two, there are ways to monetize your hobbies or passions and turn them into businesses. Make a list of them and put them on the back burner for now because we'll be coming back to them.

Let's summarize.

You have asked yourself emphatically what you don't want to do, and as a result of this, you've given yourself some insight into what you do want to do. You've focused on the experiences you want and made a list of them. You've also considered people you admire and envy and made a list of the qualities you admire. Finally, you've considered the activities you love that might be considered non-work-related.

With this list of factors and the deep consideration you've made, it's time to ask yourself the question. What kind of life do I want? What are the ideal scenarios for my career? And then ask yourself, is what I'm doing now matching what I want to do? If it's not, where are the gaps?

By now, you'll have a much clearer idea of what you want from life. You'll know whether starting your own business will fit in with your ideal routine. If answering these questions brought you to the conclusion that having your own business might not be an ideal fit for you, I am happy to have been able to help you reach this conclusion.

I suspect this exercise only whet your appetite for the business possibilities ahead. These were the key points for me when making the decision to start my own business. More importantly, they helped me keep at it in the first, difficult years, despite the negative feedback from some family members.

I liked the freedom and the lifestyle my business affords me. I liked the ability to set my own hours; even when those hours are long, they're still in my control.

I liked working on the topics of businesses that interest me the most. I liked the income and the potential for more. I also liked helping people advance their lives, which is one of the reasons I have written this book. I'm not bragging for the sake of bragging. I want you to see what's possible, but you have to take the time to see it before you build it.

Let's think about those questions again. What kind of life do you want? What do you want to be doing in your life? How do you want to be earning your income in your life? Does your life match these questions, and if not, how far away are you?

These are not just questions to ask yourself once. These are questions to ask yourself continually.

DECIDING WHAT BUSINESS TO GO INTO

Not having a reserve of cash is not an impediment to starting a business. This book is primarily tailored to those people who wish to start a new business, but either don't have buckets of cash to throw at it or have some disposable income but want to leave it aside for now. It's worth pointing out that, so far in my life, I know of no business requires zero expenditure. It's also a little bit of a cliché and also true that done smartly, putting money into a marketing plan or an advertising campaign could potentially accelerate your business a few weeks and months ahead of where you're. I have years of evidence to attest to this marketing strategy. I put my livelihood on it.

To be clear, we're looking at low-cost startup businesses. Hopefully, you've completed your life inventory and have decided the best way to fulfill your ambitions and dreams is to start your own business. You're ready to take your first steps towards getting your Millennial Business Authority (MBA). The life inventory was the prelude. This is where we start Step One, officially. First, let's cover some important mindset stuff. (DON'T SKIP OVER THIS NEXT SECTION!)

Be open to learning from the start and always.
Before I started my business in 2007, I spent a lot of time learning about search engine optimization, or SEO for short. SEO focuses on implementing various strategies and techniques to review, rewrite, and even redesign websites so that search engines like Google, Bing, and Yahoo, pick these websites and pages as a priority in their search results. The net of this is the site will appear at or near the top of any search and therefore be looked at by potential customers before other sites. Think about how often you look at the results on page 3 when you do a search. A study from 2014 showed 95 percent of the web traffic goes to the results on the first page of results with almost a third of the traffic going to the first listing.

It should be a critical part of anybody's online business, and it's something I became very good at. When I started, I couldn't afford an online course or any kind of course. Even then, there were hundreds of courses on this subject. But I was able to learn it for free. I would devour any article on the subject and learn any tips. By doing this, and by continual practice, I became hyper-effective at SEO.

Being open to learning implies learning from the many mistakes you will make. One of the reasons people shy away from starting their own businesses or doing anything challenging is a fear of mistakes. People tend to think of making one, two, or a thousand mistakes as failure. This kind of thinking is called catastrophizing.

If you're open to learning from your mistakes, you're immediately in the mindset of accepting the potential for success through making mistakes. This is critical because the chances of starting a new business and getting everything right from the get-go are extremely low to nonexistent. (Heavily weighted towards nonexistent.)

Be aware of (and smash) your own negative feedback loops. You may be familiar with the term "vicious circle" or even "self-fulfilling prophecy." This negative feedback loop can occur when you think you're doing something the right way, but you're not getting the results you want. Eventually, you repeat that pattern of behavior until bad results become expected. This cycle of expecting, acting, and receiving bad results is a negative feedback loop.

Pretend you're a DJ. You set a target of walking into 20 bars and hotels because you want to talk about and possibly sell your services. You prepare meticulously, making a list of venues all geographically near to each other.

You mentally prepare, understanding most people are going to say no to you. You make your first two stops. Both people say no. The trouble is, there's a big difference between preparing for rejection and being rejected.

You stop, have a cup of coffee, and start to go through all the other things you could be doing instead. You think, "I'll try again tomorrow." This is your negative feedback loop. You're going to do the same thing tomorrow, and you can't understand how to break out of it because you're not open to learning.

This is one thing that Millennials do well. We do like to beat ourselves up, blame ourselves, and describe ourselves as failures if we perceive things are going wrong.

As a prospective DJ, you now have a nasty little germ in your head, which tells you that you're no good at what you're doing, and you're not surprised nobody wants to see you.

The next time you try looking for new business, with these ideas locked in your mind, people sense it, and your strike rate gets even worse. This is the feedback loop, the vicious circle, and it's a self-fulfilling prophecy because if you perceive yourself as not good enough, you'll unconsciously look for events and reactions that confirm your own negative self-beliefs.

But, it doesn't have to be this way. It doesn't matter where all that crap in your head, all that negative self-talk, comes from; books about that stuff litter bookshelves across the world. What matters is that you must believe in the truth – **and the truth is, all those negative thoughts only exist in your head. They are not real.** They are constructs of your upbringing and repeated negative views of yourself.

When you grasp that negative thoughts are mere constructs, this means that you can rebuild them. You can change what you feel about yourself, and consequently, change what you do. This is an important truth.

What you think has a direct impact on what you do. I'm talking about the link between the negative feedback loop and being open to learning. If you're not open to learning, you just continue to believe you're a failure, and not cut out for whatever it is you're doing. Please, please, be kind to yourself. These negative views are wrong.

Being open to learning means taking a cool, dispassionate look at what you're doing, assessing whether there are things you can change, and coming up with new ideas. I guarantee you, if you're open to learning this way and you don't beat yourself up, results will come.

Here's a quick tip on how to remove yourself from this negative feedback loop, to turn it into a positive feedback loop, to turn your vicious circle of behavior into a virtuous circle, and yes, to still have self-fulfilling prophecies, but ones that predict success and not failure. It's all about learning you don't have to be perfect.

If you view your mistakes as the learning opportunities they are and then ensure you learn from them (because you're open to learning), you're going to go along way. No matter where people are in their lives, they make mistakes, and sometimes what differentiates the failed businessperson from the successful one is how they respond to these mistakes.

Let's look at Thomas Edison, one of the most prolific inventors of any era you can imagine. It is said Edison went through over 10,000 versions of the electric lightbulb before getting it correct.

Edison said this rather wonderful thing when talking about the entire process. "I have not failed 10,000 times. I have not failed once. I have succeeded in proving those 10,000 ways will not work. When I have eliminated the ways that will not work, I will find a way that will work" (Furr, 2011).*

Wonderful advice for your new business. Mistakes are for learning, not for being downcast. I want to close this section by giving you some nine tips on getting out of your negative feedback loop using the previous example of becoming a DJ.

1. **Just do it anyway.** Go into those 20 as you promised you would. Don't worry about your feelings and insecurities, just do it already.

2. **Set yourself a target.** Focus on achieving the target and nothing else. Switch every other noise in your head off.

3. **Take credit for happy accidents.** Life can be wonderful and can present you with through some beautiful coincidences your way, but only if you're out there looking for them. You may walk into a bar and be asked to talk to somebody about their PA or DJ needs, and the person may say, "That's interesting. I've just had my DJ cancel for tomorrow, what have you got to offer?" Boom. You're in. I'm not talking about Fantasyland here. Happy accidents like this happen all the time, but only if you're out there trying.

4. **Fake it till you make it.** It's a little bit of a cliché, but honestly, if you go into a scenario acting as if you're the answer to your potential customer's problems, you (whether deep down you believe it or not) will achieve more success. With practice, not only will you be acting as if you have a right to be there, but you will start believing you have a right to be there because your success will provide the evidence.

43

5. **Plan each activity.** Plan when you're going to see somebody and schedule it, plan what you're going to say. Plan what you want to get from each potential customer encounter. Even if, at the end of the transaction, the only thing you've got is the name of the person you need to contact (in other words, the person who makes the decision), then you achieve something. You have something.

6. **Plan your follow-up call.** Don't just leave it there. If you call to speak with someone and receive an email address from an assistant instead, schedule in your calendar when you're going to send an email and schedule when you're going to follow up the email with a call or another email. If you walk into a venue to speak to somebody and the person's not there, but you learned when the person is more likely to be there, put it in your calendar when you're going to follow through. If you let your schedule dictate your actions, you're less likely to fall into a negative feedback loop from constantly overcoming inertia.

7. **Learn, learn, learn.** This is important. Think about everything you've done. What did you learn, and what could you do better? If, for example, you're telephoning around to get business for your new DJ-ing business (I could use any business to illustrate this point), but you're getting knocked back every time, and this happens repeatedly, this doesn't mean you're a failure. This means you successfully identified the people you

want to do business with that don't like getting phone calls willy-nilly. It's up to you to try a different approach.

8. **Don't go looking for the "perfect" approach before doing something.** This is another classic mistake. Many people are afraid to do things until they've got it perfect, not realizing it doesn't matter whether it's perfect or ignoring the fact that there's no such thing as perfect. Just because you did something wrong or not completely sure how to do something shouldn't prevent you from doing it. Work out what you currently consider the best way to do something, then do it. It's not just because you're starting out in business that you won't find perfection. If it doesn't work out, try something else. You haven't failed, you've successfully identified how NOT to do something. Just like Edison.

9. **Be kind to yourself.** Keep plugging away, keep learning, keep changing things up when you think it's appropriate until you find the way that succeeds for you.

I appreciate the above advice may seem a little bit premature. After all, you haven't even chosen your business yet. But it's not. You must understand that you'd be extremely lucky if everything you wanted to do resulted in you getting everything you wanted to get straight away. Life isn't like that, at least not for most people. When you've chosen your business, review the above list and keep them in mind.

Let's get back to working out how to find the right business or businesses for you.

Start with the lowest hanging fruit

I adore this expression, but maybe you're not familiar with it. It's a rather beautiful metaphor for the vast arena of opportunities lying in front of you. You will have an immediate advantage if you start with one of those opportunities that are the most accessible to you; in other words, the "lowest hanging fruit." It gives you an opportunity for an immediate win with a set of people you know or an industry, sector, or niche you're familiar with. But what could be a definition of a low-hanging fruit opportunity? They are:

Something you could jump into straight away and make some money.

Something that won't cost you a fortune to get into.

Something in which you have some degree of knowledge or expertise.

You don't have to be the world's biggest expert. You just have to know how to do something other people need and will pay you for.

It's to your advantage if it's something you enjoy doing, but that's not a deal-breaker. You're looking to become an entrepreneur, and while the luxury of doing only things you enjoy may be realizable for some, for most, that's a longer-term aspiration. The priority here is to start a business that could give you quick financial wins.

How do you go about working out what your own low-hanging fruits are? To start, either get yourself a pen and paper or open an excel spreadsheet in your device of choice. Full disclosure. I am a spreadsheet man through and through.

I love them. I love them for their simplicity and their ability to organize tens, hundreds, even thousands of items, and dozens of different aspects of both my business and personal life. If you've got some other preferred method, good for you, but from now on, I'm going to refer to spreadsheets quite a lot. Once you've opened your spreadsheet:

Create a list of all the areas you've worked in, have knowledge of, are trained in, or simply enjoy. Include every industry, every sector, every niche. Before we go on, it's worth providing a quick definition of some of these words.

Industry. Once, this would have meant the companies or entities responsible for manufacturing and distributing a product. That definition still holds, but the word's meaning has been widened to include more abstract concepts such as the fitness industry or the comedy industry.

Sector. A word often used interchangeably with the word industry, but with a slightly different meaning. While industry can be very specific in describing a set of companies who make similar products or deal with similar segments (for instance 24-Hour Fitness and Anytime Fitness are both health clubs in the fitness industry), the term sector describes a large segment of the economy, for instance, the soft drinks sector.

Niche. A term which relates to products, services, or interests focus on and appeal to a specialized section of the population. For instance, in the fitness industry, a niche might be personal training services or elliptical cross-training machines. A niche of the soft drinks section could be sugar-free soda or mixers for alcoholic drinks.

Back to our list. It is vital to include everything, including some of the things you do for hobbies or for fun. (I told you I'd come back to it!) You may love off-road cycling. Are you a member of a club? Do you go on tours? Do you know much about the bicycles themselves, where to locate them, how to soup them up, how to repair them? What about clothes? Do you love them, are you fully acquainted with the ranges at your disposal? Another example, do you like movies and can you write reasonably well? You could consider combining these two concepts and writing movie reviews. There are literally thousands of reviewers out there, but most of them are tragically bad at it. If you can make your reviews stand out, you might be able to make money from it. In short, if you feel you have the knowledge or skillsets to monetize your hobby, be brave and stick it on your list.

In your next column, write down the names of people from each category who you know. These people should either be good immediate prospects if you're starting your own business or people who could refer business to you over the long-term.

Now, you have a list of possible businesses for your startup, and a list of promising immediate prospects to get your business off to a flying start.

This is an example from a colleague of mine, Terence, who went through this exercise and has very kindly allowed me to print some of it, with the names of people removed for obvious reasons. I'm going to be referring to Terence quite a bit.

Terence's Low-Hanging Fruit List

Area/Industry/Niche	Rating	Contacts	Title
Call center telephony	4/5	XXXXXXX	1. CEO Telephony Supplier
		XXXXXXX	2. CEO Contact center Consultancy
Boxing Equipment	1/5	XXXXXXX	1. Head of YYYY gyms
Writing Tuition	3/5	XXXXXXX	1. Head of YYYY college
		XXXXXXX	2. Head of YYYY academy
		XXXXXXX	3. Head of YYYY college
DJ/PA Equipment Hire/Sales	4/5	XXXXXXX	1. Head of YYYY hotel chain.
Computer Repairs	3/5	XXXXXXX	1. Freelance Computer Geek (his words, not mine)
Cycling Repairs	1/5	XXXXXXX	1. Owner of YYYY Bicycles & Repairs

This is not his complete list, and in some cases, as well as removing the names, I have shortened the contact list. For instance, the longest list was for a set of training centers and bars in the local area that he knew occasionally hired PA equipment. Some other observations about this list.

1. Terence graded each topic out of 5. Five being a sure-fire way of making money, and 1 being avoided like the

plague. Call-center telephony scored one of the highest because it was his main expertise (it was part of his current role, and he knew how the top five telephony systems in the country worked in detail), and he also knew selling one of these systems could be incredibly lucrative. On the smaller systems, the ticket prices were low with high margins, and on the larger systems, the ticket prices were high with reduced margins. Plus, his contacts were good, and at least one of them had in the past reached out to him to work together.

2. Terence loved boxing, at least the training aspect of it, and he wrote this down because it was a major hobby (the same applied to cycle repairs). But as he knew little about the business aspect of things, and his contacts were weak, he graded it low. "Just because I like movies," he said to me, "doesn't mean I could make one."

3. Terence had acquired some PA equipment and had occasionally DJed at various parties and clubs. Not only did he like this business, but he'd also made efforts to speak with some people, and got a positive response. The head of a large hotel chain, in particular, had told him they were crying out for good PA equipment to rent at reasonable prices. This particular person happened to be Terence's brother-in-law too.

What does your list look like? It will no doubt be different to this list, but hopefully, you will have a good idea of your lowest hanging fruit. My three main areas were Search Engine Optimization, Social Media Ads, especially Facebook and Instagram, and web design. I knew I would be able to make money from these areas.

I want you to notice something, though. Although the skills in my three areas dovetailed, what I offered were distinct and discrete from each other. In other words, I was running three separate businesses. It doesn't matter whether they were run from three separate locations (of course they weren't, would have made no financial sense at the time), and it doesn't matter whether they were registered as three separate businesses. From what I had to do, and from almost all my customers, they were three separate entities.

At the start of your business career, that's absolutely fine. You could have just one or a dozen low-hanging fruits. As long as you can devote a specific amount of time per week to each fruit, and as long as those fruits can earn you money to start with, it's all good.

For me, it was important to embark on a multiple-business approach because I wanted to learn which one would make me the most money and which would make me the happiest.

As time progressed, I rationalized my options, and my main forte nowadays is social media advertising, particularly Facebook. You will start to rationalize too, but for now, the more fruit in your basket, the more opportunities you have to make money.

Four considerations

When deciding on which fruit to pick, there are four considerations. How much money is it going to cost you to get into them? How quickly can you earn income from them? How much time will you need to devote to them to make it work for you? How much will I enjoy these activities?

When you're starting, though, you should have the enjoyment of the activities on your list as the last consideration. The priority should be how quickly you can make money from it; the second, its starting costs; and the third, how much time it will need.

If you think the chances are low, you're going to make much money from it, in the short- or long-term, then you should probably scrap the idea. Or if you think you could make money in the long-term, but not the short, put it on the backburner. The whole point of these low-hanging fruits is for you to start earning revenue as quickly as possible.

If you think it's going to cost you a lot more than anticipated to get into, it would be an important consideration too. Or if you think it's going to take you almost all your week, possibly longer, to make any money, then that might influence your decision.

If you think you're not going to enjoy the activity, but it scores high on the other factors, then you might want to get into it anyway. Later on, when you've established yourself a bit more, and you have a clearer idea of how each of your business strands fit into each other, you can look at ways of a) either moving away from a task you don't like because you're making enough money from tasks you enjoy, or b) delegating the bits you don't like, either by employing somebody to do those aspects of the task you dislike or passing the work on to somebody else – for a fee of course. This is all about the relationships you build, and we'll come back to that later in the book.

Here's a summary of the decisions above with respect to each activity. I call this the "Yes" table, because the more yeses you have, the easier the decision to dive in should be.

Activity number	Can I make quick money from it?	Will it be low-cost to start up?	Can I do it well in a short amount of time per week?	Will I enjoy it?
1	Yes	Yes	Yes	Yes
2	Yes	Yes	Yes	No
3	Yes	No	Yes	Yes
4	No	Yes	Yes	Yes

Activity 1. No-brainer. Get started.

Activity 2. Still, a no-brainer to start, but it may be an activity you drop once you get going and make enough money from all your activities. But this could take a year, two, or maybe even longer. I stopped enjoying SEO fairly quickly but kept it on for quite a while because it was a good income stream for me.

Activity 3. That NO there is quite a big one. Either you can't go into it because you don't have any money to spare, or you have some savings you're reluctant to risk. This one might be a back-burner situation. Figure out how much you will need to start it properly and then make a goal because everything else about it looks great.

Activity 4. Similar to Activity 3. What's the point in diverting your attention to an activity that isn't making you much money to start with, no matter how much you enjoy it? In this case, you can leave it for now or even turn it into a nice hobby from which you make a little extra cash.

Terence Again

Terence landed on three main fruits, call center telephony, DJ and PA equipment hire (all one aspect of his business), and computer repairs. He used his own scoring system, which was similar in subject to the one above. A score of 1 was the worst and 5 the best. Here's how some of his assessments looked, in his own words.

Call center telephony. How much money is it going to cost me to get to? 2 – Low.

How quickly can I make money from doing this? 5 – High chance.

How much time will I need to make to devote to them? Initially quite a bit, but it should settle down. 3 – Medium

How much would I enjoy doing this? There's some of it I don't enjoy, and some I do. 3 – Medium.

DJ and PA equipment hire. How much money is it going to cost me to get into? Not much, I already have a pretty decent set of equipment. I might need a few new bits. 4.

How quickly can I make money from doing this? Very quickly. I've already been asked whether I can do four consecutive Saturday nights at a hotel. 5 – High.

How much time will I need to devote to this? Not sure at this stage. Apart from ensuring the equipment is working and the transporting of it, not sure about the marketing. 3 – A guess.

How much will I enjoy doing this? I hate doing it. I don't mind playing the music, but I hate lugging the equipment, driving 50 miles, doing my thing, and then driving back. It's usually a very late finish, so I'm exhausted the next day. 1 – Poor.

Computer repairs. How much money is it going to cost me? I do need to invest in a little bit of new equipment but will source it secondhand. The initial outlay will probably cost me the equivalent of four separate repairs. 3 – Fair.

How quickly can I make money from doing this? Fairly quickly, especially because the local computer store has closed and there's currently nowhere else for miles does repairs. 4 – Good.

How much time can I devote to this? This is all completely in my control. It normally takes 2 to 3 hours to fix a computer. If I go all day, I can do four, maybe five, which will make me somewhere between $400 and $550. 4 – Good.

How much would I enjoy it? I don't love it, nor do I hate it. It's a means to an end. 3 – Fair.

Terence had identified what areas he could make money from, how quickly and how much effort it would take.

He had even identified those areas he liked and those areas he didn't like. He had discovered, for example, he didn't particularly like computer repair and long-term he didn't want to do it. Plus, he hated the DJing aspect of things but recognized its ability to make money. In the process, almost all his businesses took unexpected turns.

How to niche

Let's go back to the word "niche." You may remember it's defined as a term that relates to products, services, or interests focus on and appeal to a specialized section of the population.

This could potentially be important to you, particularly if your chief interest is in an extremely wide industry or sector. At a party recently, I heard a man declare to his colleagues he worked in the Drinks Industry. But what did he mean? Did he own a club or bar? Did he supply drinks to people, or did he manufacture or bottle them? When I asked him, it turned out he owned a factory that made those fancy cocktail shakers made famous in a film by Tom Cruise in the 1980s. Now, what was it called? Ah yes, *Cocktail*.

To guess what the man did in the drinks industry would be extremely difficult. But there's his narrowly-defined niche – making cocktail-shakers.

When you look at your list, you may have already narrowed down exactly what it is you want to get into. Just in case you haven't, there are ways to do it that don't take too long.

Let's apply this to the real world, but to a hypothetical (but realistic) example. Let's say you're into fitness. Maybe you love fitness equipment, which may be thought of as a niche but, for the purposes of this exercise, a very wide one.

You could make another list, dividing fitness equipment into smaller categories. This process is known as sub-niching or niching down. Your list might look like this:

- Cardiovascular machines

- Resistance equipment

- Free weights

Now, we have three large niches. Let's break them down even more.

Cardiovascular Machines

- Running or walking machines

- Rowing machines

- Cross-trainers, also known as elliptical trainers

- Indoor or stationary bicycles

- Stairmasters, also known as stair climbers

Resistance Equipment

- Leg presses

- Hack squats

- Leg curls

- Seated calf raises

- Standing calf raises

- Pectoral development

For brevity, I have not included the whole spectacular range of machinery, and I'm not going to complete a list of free weights. I think you get the picture on how the process of niching down is done.

Let us sub-niche one last time. This time on stationary bicycles. There are three popular sub-types.

- Standard stationary bicycles
- Recumbent bicycles, for those people with joint problems who prefer hard but lower impact exercise
- Spinning bicycles, specifically for spin classes

I could go down even further into each separate category, but there's a point (and you will know when you're there) to stop. If your business idea is generalized, it will immediately become apparent which niches are better for you. Your contacts will also be able to help you with this, and they will inform you about which ones are the lowest hanging fruit.

This exercise is useful to start with, only if you're not completely certain of the best place to apply your talents. It may also be that the lowest hanging fruit could be ALL gym equipment, and that's perfectly fine.

But dividing products down into niches is an incredibly useful exercise for several other reasons. It means you can identify markets, research into them, and find out just how much competition you have.

You've explored your life inventory and identified how self-fulfilling prophecies work for you or against you. You've spreadsheeted your business ideas, rated them and niched down to an area to focus on. The one area left in getting started right is about you, the people from whom you get further guidance. We'll call them mentors.

FINDING MENTORS

One of the most popular pieces of advice for anybody starting out in a new business is to identify and enlist the help of a mentor.

It's great advice. Having the right mentor can be an incredibly rewarding process. A mentor can act as a counselor, a teacher, an advisor, and an encourager. A mentor can be somebody in your corner, even if other people aren't.

It should be somebody you can go to for insight and advice geared specifically to your sector or niche, or your business setup. In an ideal world, your mentor can provide you with shortcuts to realizing and attaining your short-, medium-, and long-term goals. The big question is: where do you find a mentor? How do you go about even looking? Here are some tips:

- **Network, network, network.** On the surface, for somebody young and new to business, this advice can sound a little frustrating. For emerging entrepreneurs, it's difficult to know where to start networking. Yes, you're aware networking helps you build important connections and can be a vital cog in procuring new business, but how do you go about it?

- **Look to your own network first.** I'm not just talking about your business contacts. Look at your family. Think about your circle of friends. First, the ones you meet face-to-face. Then, look at your Facebook friends, because if you're like me, you'll have a small group of people you call friends and a huge bank of other people you've "friended" on Facebook. Include Instagram, Twitter, Snapchat, and all the other social media outlets you use.

- **Study your network for potential mentors. (Include your low-hanging fruit contacts.)** Chances are, if you're looking for a mentor in your own basket of low-hanging fruit opportunities, you may have somebody already tailor-made for the role. As an example, you've already made a list of people who are going to help you break into making your own money. Look at this list again. Is there anybody on this list who might fit the profile? Remember, **you're looking for somebody who can counsel you, school you, advise you, encourage you, who can be in your corner, who can provide you with shortcuts to expanding your business, and who can help you make more money.** It's quite a list of qualities. Don't discount the idea there may be a mentor who can help you with learning new aspects of business, and one who can help you with taking on new staff. At this stage, don't worry if you identify more than one person.

- **Concentrate first on making connections.** To start with, it might be difficult to find a one-size-fits-all person. When you look at the network you have, you might want to consider the best way to build connections with a variety of people rather than finding this elusive super mentor. That's why it's important to look at the people you want to do business with but who are not necessarily going to be customers.

- **Don't confine yourself to your own field.** If you can find somebody who you get along with, who can teach you things will help with your business, and who is willing to share his or her insights, it doesn't matter what business they're from, you've got a potential mentor.

- **Keep expanding your network.** Look at expanding your network. To do this, you already started with your list of people within your own network, perhaps ask them if they know like-minded people who may be in the same business. Then, go on the hunt for networking groups, small business forums, etc. You will find some of these on your social media networks, just do a search. You'll find them online, but you'll also find them advertised in various community areas like libraries. Look on Meetup sites. If you don't see anything you like, start your own meet-up group.

- **Go to any relevant events you can find.** There is no substitute for immediate face-to-face contact. There might be a seminar on an aspect of your business, new technology to learn about, or changes in your industry that concern the future of your business. Maybe a well-known local businessperson is doing a speech. Go to the website of your competitors or people within your field. You might find the events you can attend.

- **If you go to any of these things, be prepared.** You might learn some new stuff that's going to help you in your business, but your primary purpose here is to build your whole network, as well as keep your eye out for a mentor. If you have business cards, have a band of them with you, and be prepared to give them out. Just as importantly, ask people for their business cards, and when you finish a conversation, if you find somebody who you think will be helpful to you in the future, make a little note on the back of the card, particularly if you think it's worth contacting this person straightaway. In Chapter 5, Forge Productive Relationships, we're going to go into detail about a methodology for you to build your network and what to do with all your prospective contacts.

- **Don't wait too long.** Here's the key thing, if you've met somebody who you think could provide some mentoring for you and you think might be interested, you've broken the ice, you've met them, and you've had a chat with them. Don't wait too long. You must strike while the iron is hot. You've had a great chat with somebody, swapped business cards, and suggested you get in touch (if they're receptive to it), if you leave it for any more than a week, then a warm opportunity will probably go cold.

- **Become a member of relevant professional associations.** You may find a whole range of people who may suit your needs. From his telephony career, Terence joined the United States Telecom Association, US telecom. They covered every single aspect of telecommunications and telephony you could think of – all the software, hardware, training, even relevant furniture. If you join a group of this nature, especially if you attend events, you will be exposed to people who have been successful and who have perhaps achieved the level of success you're aiming for. You'll find people who are not necessarily competitors to you as well, which will make them potentially more receptive to mentoring as there's no direct competition. To check out these kinds of associations that are relevant to your business, look on the website careeronestop.org.

- **Use other online resources.** There is LinkedIn or MicroMentor.org, a site which connects small business with mentees for free. Your local Small Business Association is a helpful resource. Through them, you may be able to find a SCORE.org mentor.

- **Do a Google search.** Although there are other search engines out there, like Bing or Yahoo, Google has captured nearly 90% of the search engine market. Whatever you're looking for will be on there. In your Google search, type in "courses in [your particular sector, niche or industry/industry]". Do another search, this time stating, "top experts in [your niche/sector/industry]". The results should provide you with a list of websites mention the most popular, important, or successful people in the field you've searched in.

- **Start researching these people.** Seek out their Facebook, Instagram, Twitter, or any other social media they have attached themselves to. Read reviews, particularly online reviews from people who have used their services or products. These kinds of reviews are known as social proof and provide a fantastic insight into the people you're searching for.

- **Don't be afraid to ask.** You have done all this work, and you may have identified somebody you think would be an ideal mentor. Or maybe you've identified somebody who is in your business, who you see as almost being in a different stratosphere. If you don't ask, you won't get. Ask if they would consider offering advice on an aspect of your business. They can only say no, and even if they do say no, I'm willing to bet you, they will say no in an incredibly constructive way from which you will learn. You might be surprised. People love helping other people. In my experience, successful people love helping other people to achieve success.

What to do with your potential new mentor

- Invite them for a coffee and a chat. Ask them about their business and themselves. Take time to get to know them. First and foremost, develop the relationship.

- Don't use the word mentor, at least to start with. The word "mentoring" implies a big commitment. I'm not suggesting you be underhanded. If somebody offers you advice and teaches you something that will help your business, that's mentoring. If they're happy doing it, then it's fine.

- Ask. If you do want somebody to be a full-on mentor, if you built a relationship for them and you're comfortable, ask them when you're certain they're going to say yes. Because if you treat somebody as a mentor but you have failed to inform them. Eventually, you'll damage the relationship. It's best to be upfront.

- Try to use somebody who is not closely linked to your business. There are two reasons for this. If it's somebody who is in the same business as you, there could be an element of competition. But also, a person who doesn't have close links to your business either emotionally or financially may be in a better position to be as objective as they need to be and maybe more brutally honest with you than somebody with those links, who might not be as upfront.

- Be somebody worth mentoring. Look the part, act professionally, and if you ask somebody for a card and say you're going to contact her, follow it up. Do your homework about your mentor and work hard. If you say you're going to do something, do it. There's nothing less professional if you don't stick to commitments. It will make a potential or an actual mentor run away from you.

- Be a sponge and genuinely interested. Listen attentively to what your mentor has to say. Show real interest. They are more likely to give you more information about how they did something. If you're not interested, it will become apparent very quickly.

- Never pay for mentoring. Yes, some people charge for their mentoring. But there is a massive difference between somebody who is being paid to mentor and one who does it because they want to.

- You scratch my back, I'll scratch yours. A mentor is somebody who's doing you a huge favor, and that's something you shouldn't take lightly. As well as letting them know how much you appreciate them, offer them something in return. What you offer could be business-related, such as referrals. Or it could just be simple simply saying, "Look. If you ever need to talk to me about something, I'm always there for you." The best relationships are ones where people help each other.

- Establish clear boundaries. It's important everybody understands what your relationship is all about, what specific topic you're working towards your mentor is helping you with. Also, things like how many times you meet, emails, or telephone calls can be agreed too.

- Finally, your mentor is not you. Whatever advice they give you comes directly from their own perspective. Sure, sometimes what your mentor says fits exactly with what you need or want, but there are other times when it's perfectly acceptable to be grateful for the counsel given to you by your mentor but not necessarily follow it or even to discount it completely. This isn't going to happen very often. Remember – **you are you, and your business is your business.** Both are unique.

Your mentor is not your boss and does not own your company.

Terence's mentoring experience

For Terence, his business went off in interesting directions because he was on the lookout. He went into a PA equipment center and started talking to a shopper in the store. It turned out the gentleman he was talking to was a booking agent. People contacted his business to book acts, equipment, and everything else.

What he said he was missing was anybody with equipment. That's the direction piqued Terence's interest. He started procuring more equipment and hiring it out.

On the advice of the shopper, he also developed a bank of DJs and public speakers, some of whom had their own equipment, some of whom didn't. Not only did he start booking equipment rentals, but he also started booking acts. This all came about because of a chance meeting and the fact both parties were open to discussion.

Terence's temporary mentor, in this instance, worked in a different part of the U.S., so there was limited competition. What he also offered was to refer business to Terence – in return for a cut. This proved to be a very fertile relationship, and the gentleman in question was able to give Terence some fantastic advice, thus boosting his earnings.

CHAPTER 2

Step 2 – The Three Ps of Longevity

TERENCE AND MONEY

Before we get into the three Ps, it's time for a Terence update. Here is how Terence started making money.

Telephony

Incidentally, he worked in an IT department of a large customer service company who had contact centers dotted around the country. That's why he knew so much about call center telephony. He was particularly knowledgeable about one call telephony system. The CEO of another company who had installed the system had even approached his boss intending to second him (for a fee) to instigate training. His boss had said no, but not before he had shared all the information he had with Terence, including how much the other company was willing to pay for Terence's services. It was a princely sum.

He came up with a plan, and yes, there was a little bit of underhandedness to it. He decided to take a two-week vacation and then add two weeks of unpaid leave on top of it. He didn't tell his company why. He wasn't quite ready to quit his job yet – he wanted to see how things went and how much money he could make. He independently approached the CEO and offered to complete the training over four weeks at three different sites.

Knowing what the CEO was willing to offer his boss, he went in at price. Instinct told him the CEO would barter him down, and in his head, he was willing to go down to 60%. It was still a large amount of money for very little outlay. All he had to source was a cheap printer to print off handouts, but most of it was going to be on an online portal he had created for the training to be completed at the company's premises.

It turned out the CEO did barter him down, but only to 75%. In four weeks, he was set to make a profit of around $9,000. The payment was a good enough start for him.

DJ/PA Equipment

He contacted and took the booking for four Saturdays, which was to start almost immediately after his training would be completed. From this, he made a profit of $1,800. Not bad for four nights' work and a couple of days' preparations.

Computer Repairs

Terence put together some flyers at a relatively low cost and posted them in the usual places. He created a Facebook page that didn't get an enormous amount of traffic to start with, but he pointed all his friends at it and then waited for the queries to come in. He made the sensible decision of not doing any of this until towards the end of his training course, which took him away from home anyway. This was a sensible decision because to start with, the whole thing was busy immediately, and he ended up spending three days a week repairing other peoples' PCs from the back of his apartment. He made an average profit of $100 a repair, mostly because the repairs were complex and centered around higher-end items like laptops.

Terence had got off to a flying start, which brought some problems. He decided to quit his job and was faced with an immediate dilemma. His boss offered him a dramatic pay raise. He said no, and then his boss offered to allow him to work two days per week at a higher rate. He thought long and hard about and said no because he was buoyed by the immediate success of his three business areas.

That was a decision he would come to partially regret. For now, let's get back to those three Ps.

WHAT ARE THE THREE PS?

Businesses can sometimes be a very complex beast with many different facets to it. Or is it? I think sometimes business people like to create the illusion of complexity when the most effective businesses keep things as simple as possible.

The concept of practice, patience, and persistence is one of those incredibly simple but incredibly effective principles you should repeat to yourself, and stick to, on an ongoing basis. It's not rocket science. It's business sense.

Before we get into the three Ps of longevity, I want to briefly touch upon another important P – planning.

Planning

The consensus amongst top business folk is you should plan any business up to a minimum of five years ahead and possibly longer.

But for Millennials, the idea of planning five years ahead and being able to stick to the plan seems almost laughable. Here's why:

1. We live in far less secure times. The business environment changes rapidly.

2. It's the changes in technology that are driving many business changes, and as many businesses rely almost totally on technology, planning five years ahead seems almost redundant.

3. Following the advice in this book means you want to make a head start as an entrepreneur by plucking off your low-hanging fruit opportunities. The chances of you continuing with all those business strands reduce as time passes. Let me give you my own example. As I've already mentioned, I started with search engine optimization (SEO). It's not something I particularly enjoyed, but it was something I was good at. These days, I don't touch it.

I'm not suggesting you do no plans at all, that's even worse. Having no plans and no goals are, in my opinion, a surefire way to fail in business. What I have done, and what I am suggesting you do is to plan for the next 12 months. Then, break your plan down into three-month increments, detailing what you want to achieve in the next 3, 6, 9, and 12 months. Review every three months. This is just as motivating (if not more motivating) than a remote 5- to 10-year plan because you're living it in real-time.

How did Terence do?

You may recall Terence decided on three strands to his starting business, call center telephony, DJ and PA equipment hire, and computer repairs. Crucially, Terence didn't bother with a plan, at least to start with.

And boy, what a start he had. He picked up a lucrative training contract for the telephony side of his business, and this was before he had even left his current role. He picked up another weekly DJ contract that brought him in $1,800 of profit for four nights spread over a month.

Due to the coincidence of a local computer repair shop closing, what he thought would be the quietest part of his business, initially at least, became the busiest and was repairing other peoples' PCs. He was repairing three days a week and averaged five repairs a day over four weeks. He was making $8,000 in the first month alone. Most of his computer repair business came from a flyer he produced at a relatively low cost and distributed himself around businesses in the local area.

From a financial and activity perspective, the first three months of his business looked like this:

Month One. Four-week training program for a new telephone system. Total profit of $8,000.

DJing – Total profit of $9,000

Month Two. Repair of 62 printers and PCs, an average profit of $100 per item. Total profit of $6,000.

Two more nights of DJing – Total profit $750.

But let's look at months three and four.

Month Three. 18 computer repairs, an average profit of $82 (items had begun to get smaller). Total earnings – $1,476.

Telephony and DJ/PA Businesses – No money made.

Month Four. Three repairs totaling profit of $245. Once again, no money was made in Telephony and the DJ/PA Business.

There are two reasons why there was such a huge fall-off in revenue. The first one is because Terence didn't have a plan in place. Specifically, he had no idea how much money he needed to earn, whether it be to cover his personal bills or for the business.

With no plan in place, he blindly went on with his busy lifestyle. He couldn't see the forest for the trees. In a way, getting such a hot-off-the-blocks start for Terence poisoned the well for him. He had just assumed the business was going to be easy to acquire.

In another way, it did him a massive favor because he realized he needed a plan. The second reason why Terence's revenue dropped off a cliff is that he hadn't followed the three Ps. It's the three Ps of longevity that brought him down off the ledge, a figure of speech, of course. The next stage after his plan was for Terence to translate the three Ps into specific, money-earning actions. We'll come back to Terence later in this chapter. It's time to look at the first P of longevity.

PRACTICE

The simplest way to become good at something is to practice it over and over. Yes, it's a cliché, but practice makes perfect is an undeniable truism. As is the less well-known but equally pertinent saying, "practice makes permanent." If you practice something enough, it lodges permanently in your brain and becomes second nature.

Why practice is good for your business

Practice has three big impacts. First, you get better at what you practice. That's all there is to it. What's even more important is that you get better at doing it the way that you practice. If you practice a bad process, you'll improve at doing it badly and vice versa. Second, practicing helps you replace old habits with new habits. From a business perspective, particularly if you've moved on from working for somebody else, practicing your entrepreneurial skills and the diverse range of things you have to do helps you develop good habits, provided you consider and reflect upon everything you do.

Working for somebody else requires a specific mentality and gets you into habits that work in the employee arena. I'm not criticizing this path, but you're the product of your environment.

Working for yourself requires a shifting base of habits, shifting viewpoints, and a more flexible mentality. By continually practicing all aspects of being a small business owner and attempting to do them well, you're capturing new, increasingly productive habits for yourself.

Finally, you get into the habit of developing new habits. That's going to be vital because your business, particularly in the low-hanging fruit stage, is going to go through some tumultuous changes, and your behavior will have to change accordingly.

Let's just talk a bit more about these three benefits of practice, and discuss a way of kick-starting your learning and, in the process, helping your business success come more rapidly.

Practice makes you better.

Of course, it does. If you practice how to play the piano, you get better at it; if you practice how to drive, you get better at it. If you practice any aspect of your business, you get better at it. Whether you think about what you're doing or not, you will get better at doing something if you practice it repeatedly.

However, I can't stress this enough, without pausing to think about what you're doing and actively attempting to assess whether there are better ways of doing things, what you could end up potentially doing is practicing bad habits and getting better at them. You may become more efficient at doing something badly, but without pausing to think, you'll never learn better ways of doing things.

I call this the do-reflect-plan model of practicing. If you read lots of literature on this, you find it called different things. I'm not claiming to have come up with something brand spanking new and original. If I had, I'd be writing a book about that!

This is not just a way of fine-tuning your practice. It's a way of drastically improving what you're doing and giving your learning a massive shot of adrenaline. Besides, it's a brilliant way of almost immediately breaking any negative feedback loop. A cool analysis and reflection of what you're doing will provide you with insight on how to do something better almost immediately.

Let me give you a real-time example from Terence. Terence wasn't a massive fan of DJing, but for a quick cash injection, there was nothing better. Terence didn't only play music. When requested, he hosted events and even organized charity raffles. The most money he made in one evening was $1,000. All told, this was for about seven hours of work.

One day, Terence got a call from somebody who had used him before. She said to him, "I've got two venues that need filling. Do you know anybody?" He did, and he passed the details on. What a nice guy he is.

The next day, exhausted, as usual, Terence played last night in his head. He thought about his conversation with the customer and wondered what he could have done differently, and it hit him. He wondered if there was a way to outsource the work and still make some money from it. He was now in the middle of the reflection stage of his business.

Two ideas came to him. The first one was to act as a go-between – to have a bank of reputable hosts and DJs, with their own equipment, and effectively become a booking agent. He would take a percentage, around about 20% of every booking, and the rest would go to the DJ or host.

The second idea was to acquire more equipment and rent the equipment out either to venues or to other DJs. Or both. He knew this would take an investment. He couldn't afford it at the time, so he went for option one. Because he's a good guy and he was amassing a decent reputation, it was easy to attract DJs, but he made a point of seeing those DJs in action to ensure they were good, and he only put on his books the best of them. He was able to take more bookings and cherry-pick the ones he did himself. He maximized his earnings into new ways there. All from the process of practicing the do-reflect-plan model. In summary, the process goes like this:

Do. Perform the relevant action of what you're doing.

Reflect. Reflect on what you're doing, ask questions like:

Did the action go exactly as I expected?

What feedback did I get from my clients/customers?

What was different?

What went wrong?

What can I do to ensure it doesn't go wrong again?

What went right? What can I do to ensure it happens again?

What did I learn to do better?

What did I learn to stop doing?

What improvements can I make to the service/product I offer?

You may go through this process and come up with nothing, but I would be surprised if there is at least something you can't improve on or avoid doing.

Plan/change. This is where you make any new plans or make any changes to your offering. It's important to remember that when you're making a change, you record how the change went. Think about it like a scientific experiment. The best experiments are analyzed and recorded.

Do. Go back to stage one.

Repeat this process until you cannot improve anything, which will never be!

If you're in a hurry to improve your business and make more money, this process will stand you in good stead.

Practice helps you forge new healthy habits or replace old, unhealthy habits.

This is a big one because research demonstrates that old habits may suit your current situation may not suit your new role as an entrepreneur. Finances are a good example of how old habits can interfere with your new lifestyle.

Most people I know who have a decent job and salary don't have a clue, on a day-to-day basis, what's going on with their finances. They have a general idea of how much money they need to keep going, but they won't know exactly when their bills are paid and won't catch variations because they're not looking for it (for example, being charged twice for a bill). They might save; they might not.

The messy business of daily finances and how it impacts on weekly, monthly, and yearly finances is pushed under the rug. They don't think about it because they don't believe they have to unless something dramatic changes, like redundancy, or a hefty increase in outgoing bills.

Lack of focus is a habit. As a businessperson, especially an entrepreneur with several strings to your bow, these old habits have to be obliterated. You must be aware of your finances. You have to know:

- How much your monthly survival amount is (I'm going to use the monthly mode because 80% of bills usually arrive monthly. By survival, I mean the minimum amount of money you need to pay your monthly bills, including food, etc.).

- How to budget weekly, monthly, yearly, quarterly, six-monthly, yearly.

- How to differentiate between personal and business finances.

- How to keep meticulous track of everything that comes in and out of your account.

- How much to charge. When pricing potential new business, know exactly how much it's going to cost you and how much you expect to make from each piece of business.

- Return on Investment (ROI). One of the best things you can do for your future of your business is to become familiar with the concept of Return on Investment for all aspects of your business. For example, if you need to take on a member of staff, you need to know exactly how much it's going to cost you, and how much extra revenue/profit/savings you'll make in other aspects of the business. Likewise, if you buy new equipment, you need to know when or if new business is going to pay for it and how the new equipment contributes to those earnings.

- How to fill in tax returns. You need to be even more familiar with completing tax returns, especially for businesses. The best practice is to have a knowledgeable tax preparer or accountant prepare your taxes for you.

This list sounds a lot, and it's not even definitive, but honestly, don't worry. A lot of the tasks merge into each other and can be chunked into bite-size elements. And once you start getting into the daily habits of becoming aware of your finances, every aspect of it, these habits will replace the old habits of indifference.

A habit is nothing more than a repeated behavior that has created a neural pathway in your brain. This neural pathway is completely clear, which means it's something you're comfortable doing. Even if you stop and attempt to get rid of an old habit, most neuroscientist state, based on people's behavior, these old pathways or habits don't go away but remain ready to be reintroduced in the absence of a new alternative.

Consequently, doing things differently, forging new habits, creates new neural pathways on top of the old ones. And the more we practice our new habits, the stronger this neural pathway becomes. By practicing new skills, you're creating new healthy habits. That's why practice is important.

Practice gets you into the habit of forming new habits.

Very closely linked to Point 2, but so fundamentally important it deserves its own number, is that the process of learning new habits is a healthy habit itself. Practicing something new is made up of a lot of important separate points.

For example, new habits are an emotional process. When you practice something new, you're not very good at the start. That's why you're practicing. Tackle the fear of changing habits and summon up the bravery for practicing new habits.

Then, decide, which is another biological process. Practice despite feeling unsure of your new habits and despite the pull of the old, easier habits. The decision supersedes the feeling. You do it because you said you would.

Envisioning the outcome of your new habit, visualizing the process, and planning the benefits (financial, timesaving, or otherwise) is another new skill you're acquiring. Fear of failure may summon up ideas of insurmountable challenge, pain, or discomfort. You must actively create the future you want to create.

Finally, tolerating discomfort in the short-term as you change old habits for long-term gain is another skill. Your brain likes things to remain as they are because what you've done has kept you alive. It forms the comfort zone. When you step outside of that bubble of safety, your brain sends out warnings and rings alarms, which are the discomfort you feel.

Now that you know what to expect from creating new habits make practice a regular part of your business strategy. Positively changing habits is one of the best habits you can acquire, and the more you do it, the better you become at it.

How practice has worked for me

When I started running Facebook ads in 2007, it was a relatively new game. There were no manuals, no training courses, just practice – and that's what I did. Facebook ads were evolving at the same speed and pace of the Facebook platform itself was. I was able to conduct lots of little experiments at a low cost. As I practiced running these advertisements, my understanding of the platform grew. Most importantly of all, the more my ability to identify which campaigns would work and which wouldn't begin to embed in. I became very good at knowing what to advertise, where to advertise it, and when to advertise it, and that's where the lion's share of my business comes from nowadays.

I became more confident about sharing those experiences with other people, and all of this came from hours and hours of practice and hundreds and hundreds of ads. The more practice I got, the better I became, and the easier I found it to talk about. As a consequence, I got better at forging relationships and growing my network.

People recognize BS. It's an intuitive sense. When you're talking to somebody from the position of an expert based on your personal experiences, they'll also recognize the integrity of your stories. As a result of this, my customer base and my turnover grew exponentially. All from practice!

PATIENCE

Patience is one of the most underrated qualities in business. It's no wonder, with everything moving so quickly. But patience also comes once you've set reasonable expectations. Patience is indelibly linked to having realistic goals and a systematic process for achieving those goals. If you have neither of these, if you don't know what you want to achieve, and you don't know how to go about achieving it, you will soon run out of patience.

I spoke earlier about having a year-long plan or even just six months, but I like to stick to year. That's one of the other great advantages of having a year-to-year plan as opposed to a 5- or 10-year plan. A super long plan seems kind of remote, and it makes it a little harder to wed your day-to-day actions with this plan.

Don't get me wrong, I'm not decrying longer plans if they work for your business. But at the very least, either have a one-year plan or, if you have a longer plan for 5 or 10 years, translate into a realistic one-year expectation.

List the set of goals in your first year

List the set of tasks you want to achieve in your first year. It could be anything. It could be making $10,000 overall in a year, or it could be making $10,000 a month. You'll then be able to create a reasonable set of tactics to achieve whatever figure you set. Contact x amount of people. Have one, two, or ten new customers a month. Fit one new telephony system every three months. Get to grooming five dogs a day by month three. Or sell 10 new products on Amazon ongoing every month with a margin of over 30%.

As you can see, I've used a spread of objectives there because it can apply to any business type or model, whether your selling services or selling specific products. Knowing what you want to do means you can plan on a monthly, even weekly, basis, and everything you do should be in the service of all your objectives.

Create incremental goals

Let's say you figure out that to get 10 new customers a month requires you to speak or have contact with 300 people. From there, you can estimate that you can go meet 50 people, make 150 phone calls, send 100 emails. From this, you get 8 new customers. Adjust your activity for the next month to match your desire to get 10 new customers, which in turn feeds into your yearly plan. Every month, you're learning. Every month, your task is incremental. Every month, you move closer to your yearly objectives. You're patiently trying new things, and if things don't work, you're adjusting and learning.

Patience can be displayed in many ways, including accepting you're learning something new and may not get it right the first time. Understand that it may take several attempts.

Appreciate that the best way to learn something is not through a course (the courses are tremendously useful), but by doing it and having a mentor guide you. I once heard this analogy about learning to swim. The US Olympic swim team could give you ideas on strokes and the best way to do them. You may have access to the best book in the world about swimming. It tells you every single thing you need to know. But all of this will count for nothing (at least to start with) when you're standing at the edge of the deep end and somebody pushes you in.

When you learn by doing, you're going to make more mistakes; that's where the learning happens. Learn from courses and effectively apply those courses to benefit your business.

For some reason, patience is the hardest quality to retain consistently. People tend to compare themselves to other entrepreneurs and businesses, which is a surefire way to feel bad. A patient businessperson will work on changing the things they can change and not worry about the rest.

Being patient also means accepting there are some goals you're going to achieve in the timescale you set, and some you might not. Terence worked out his monthly survival fund is $4,500. He had just over $26,000 in his savings, which was just under six months of expenses.

That became his first main goal, to earn $4,500 within six months. He didn't quite get there. The figure he got to was $4,000, give or take $100. An impatient man might have given up, but Terence looked at his objectives and recalibrated.

Besides which, he hadn't blown his entire $26,000 saving because he had earned well over in the first two months.

In his quietest months, the most he had to dig into his savings was $2,000. The total amount he had to take from it was $6,000, leaving a little over $19,000. Toward the end of the six months, he managed to procure at least $4,000 of regular income for the next four months.

For context, a few months into his business, he sold his first large telephony installation, which doubled his earnings over the same four-month period. He had got to his magic figure, just a few months later than he had planned. All was good. That's what patience is about.

PERSISTENCE

"Nothing in this world can take the place of persistence. Talent will not; nothing is more common than unsuccessful men with talent. Genius will not; unrewarded genius is almost a proverb. Education will not; the world is full of educated derelicts. Persistence and determination alone are omnipotent. The slogan Press On! has solved and always will solve the problems of the human race."

— **Calvin Coolidge, US President, 1923-1929**

What exactly do we mean by persistence? Persistence is continuing to do something despite obstacles, setbacks, or opposition. It's about persevering, being tenacious, dogged, displaying stamina, and a degree of consistency as well. It is what Thomas Edison called "stick-to-itiveness."

It is as closely linked to the other two Ps – practice and patience – as it's possible to be. You could describe the three Ps as being three pillars propping up the expansion and continued success of your new business. You can't have one without the others.

If you're impatient, you're less likely to be persistent, and if you're not practicing and learning about your business, you will not move forward anywhere near as quickly (or perhaps not at all), and in case, persistence will work against you (you may be persistent, but persistently doing something wrong).

There can sometimes be a conflict between learning new things from your practice and being persistent. You may try something new, but the first time you try it, it doesn't work out. If you change it immediately after the first attempt, you could argue this is not persistent because you haven't given your new way enough of a chance.

This is a delicate balancing act, and it's wholly dependent on your business, the new thing you're working through, and your own personal experiences.

You will know yourself how many times it's worth trying something before changing it up, and it's true, sometimes you know straight away. A general rule of thumb - try something new at least three times before assessing its success or failure.

Its persistence that will make your business successful despite long odds. The going may be tough, and sometimes it can get you down, but persistence is the one quality that will enable you to keep going on even when you don't feel motivated. That's why there is such a direct relationship between persistence and success.

It's one of those feedback loops, but this time a great one. The more you persist, the more confident you will be. And the more confident you are, the more you persist. It's not just Edison who kept at it. Bill Gates, Steve Jobs, and Mark Zuckerberg (of Microsoft, Apple, and Facebook, respectively) were all college dropouts. Look at the legacy all three of them have either left or are leaving.

Persistence is its own reward. Keep at it. Keep persisting, and you will eventually succeed, leading you to want to do more.

HOW PATIENCE, PRACTICE, AND PERSISTENCE WORK TOGETHER

There are lots of people in the world who display two of these three P's and don't succeed. You may have people who are practicing, learning, and persistently applying what they learn to everything they do, but suddenly they lose patience. Maybe they don't get the number of customers they thought they would have at this stage or don't make the money they planned. All that practice and persistence will have come to nothing without patience. The three Ps need each other.

Let's go back to Thomas Edison and his numerous attempts to perfect the lightbulb. What a perfect example of all three qualities. Had he not had the desire to practice and learn, he might have given up after a few attempts. He needed patience and persistence just as much. If one of these qualities had not been present in Edison's mindset, he might not have been the first to invent the lightbulb as we know it. Clearly, he had all three qualities to the Nth degree. This is a man who has 1,000 patents to his name, more than any other American inventor, living or dead.

Other ways persistence will help your business

- It will help you achieve your goals, even if it appears as if you're not achieving them, even at the point when you're furthest away from them, because you will keep on going.

- It will help you to push through the low days. We all have had them. Unless you're an unwaveringly cheerful person (some people are, but not many, and if you're, I envy you) or a robot. I've had those days, particularly at the start of the process when I didn't have a lot of support from my family. I was also locked temporarily in what people call the feast or famine mode, where for a month or two, I had lots of work and then for the next couple of months very little. That, combined with the fact I was working hard all the waking hours I could, made me feel a bit low and vulnerable sometimes, but I kept my eyes on the prize, and I kept at it. I was persistent. The persistence helped me, and it will help you too.

- It will keep the number and quality of client list high because you keep working at it.

Terence and the Three Ps

Let's take a quick look at how Terence benefited from the three Ps.

Practice. Well, he certainly practiced while he was doing the work itself. And he learned a lot about computer repairs that he didn't know previously. He learned the hard way about planning and acquiring new business and continued to practice at both to keep in good stead.

Patience. He kind of rushed into his business. Granted, he made some good money straight away, followed by a slow period. A more patient approach might have helped.

He worked out after two months what he needed to do, and once the first two months of furious activity died down, he put his foot on the break and started planning properly for the coming months, an admirable display of learning and patience.

Persistence. While he was never to find acquiring business quite as easy as he did in those first two months, he knew it was something he would have to work hard at. In a way, what happened did him a massive favor.

The first thing he did was a six-month plan. This time he knew how much he needed to earn and survive. That number was his base figure. He also researched in all three of his areas where to get more business and planned meticulously how long he was going to spend putting himself out there networking and building up his reputation.

He also picked up some unexpected contacts for people who could help him with computer repairs. The reason he wanted to farm this out was straightforward.

Although he was indifferent to computer repairs before his busy period, he realized how much he hated doing it after repairing so many computers in such a short time. He didn't want to drop it because it brought in some healthy revenue, nor did he want to get bogged down in those exhausting finicky repairs. Sound familiar?

So, he decided to outsource some of the work. He gave 50% of what he was making to the repairer and kept 50% himself. This model was to serve him well with his PA equipment rental business, too.

He had a plan and displayed patience. He would need to draw on his reservoirs of persistence.

Why persistence is good for you

You have a much greater chance of success. I've already said this, but most companies fail when the owners or the main decision-makers give up too easily. Those business leaders who keep at it, who can plow on regardless, are the successful ones.

Persistent people and persistent businesses are more likely to be innovative. Because you won't see obstacles in your way as permanent, you treat them as hurdles to be dealt with. You become creative in working out how to get over them, finding new ways to do things and to succeed.

Persistence enhances your reputation. If you become known as somebody who doesn't give up in the face of obstacles, people will perceive you as a go-getter, somebody who wants to succeed in your businesses and wants to be the best. People are much more likely to want to do business with you and associate themselves with you in that case.

Persistence helps you discover more opportunities. This is simply because you don't give up when something is in your way. Take the salesperson out cold calling (a tough thing to do) who has a bad few calls and gives up. For all the salesperson knows, the next call could've been a golden opportunity. Had he been persistent, he would have discovered it.

Getting new business is partially a numbers game. The more persistent you are with your numbers, the more likely you are to get new business.

I firmly believe people make their own luck. Those who are the most persistent and work around obstacles don't suddenly find themselves with fabulous opportunities through chance, but because they made their own luck by keeping going. I promise you the more persistent you're, the more likely you're to get more business.

Your persistence becomes catching. Once your business grows, you will need a team. If your team sees they're working for a person who never gives up, they are more likely to mirror those attributes and work harder for you.

Persistence is an essential quality if you wish to be a successful entrepreneur or business leader, especially in today's competitive and constantly changing environment. Your persistence will set you well on the road to growing your business year-on-year and making it a stable entity

CHAPTER 3

Step 3 – Finding a Business That Suits Your Personality

PART 1: THREE BUSINESS MODELS

In this chapter, we're going identify the kind of business that suits your personality. We'll discuss different types of businesses and their common features, and follow that with details about how these businesses work, give examples of the types of businesses, and give you steps to identify for yourself which business model you prefer.

Of course, there are thousands, tens of thousands of different types of businesses out there, but they can be broken down into three categories, at least in terms of selling your products or services. Let's get straight into it.

SELLING FOR OTHERS

This is the kind of business where you won't necessarily be creating your own product or services. You sell the products or services of other people instead. Let's go back to Terence for a minute because this is where he started.

Terence's main idea was to learn everything he could about the 10 most popular contact center telephony systems in the US. He had done most of the legwork already, and his next step was to approach representatives, either from the companies directly or the distributors of products, to act as an agent for them. He was successful in seven instances, all of whom were in the top five anyway. The other companies liked him but had different ways to market. One of them even offered him a job.

Eventually, he intended to set himself up as a single agent selling these products, but to start with, he partnered with a company that offered consultancy services for all things call-center and contact-center related.

What he offered was unique because there wasn't anybody else with as much detail over such a broad span of products. The range of products he had come to know in detail were products catered for a company as small as six employees, one as big as 30,000, and everything in between.

What he did was a combination of business models. He

acted as an agent for the company's products, and, for the call center consultancy he dealt with, he sold their white label products.

White labeling is when one company uses another company's products by stripping off all the labels that would identify the original manufacturer and placing their own branding on it, effectively selling the product as if it were their own. The simplest example I can think of is self-branded breakfast cereals from Walmart and other stores. Walmart doesn't make them; big companies like Kellogg's do. Walmart puts new packaging on the cereal with the label Great Value.

The kind of individual who is happy to sell other peoples' products is also interested in what's called affiliate marketing. For example, you may have a website for a range of products. An online supplier will pay you a fee to place advertisements for their products, or to namedrop them, mention them in a blog, or any way that allows the traffic on your website to see and click on another company's products. These are the ads you see on your favorite websites.

Here's another example. If you sell fitness equipment, an ideal affiliate marketing partner for you might be national gymnasiums with branches all over the country. Maybe fitness drinks or clothing. You get the picture.

With the right agreements and done well, affiliate marketing can be a lucrative and easy way to earn extra money. The kind of content I'm talking about is direct advertisements or sponsored posts. People will write blogs or create video content where they'll mention or promote products that complement their own.

While affiliate marketing as a standalone feature belongs firmly in the camp of selling something without meeting anybody, I mention it here because it lends itself to any business model, including you leverage influencers to sell your own products by turning them into affiliates.

Back to Terence. While he started by acting as an agent or sales representative for the products he sold, he also had other aspirations. This is an important consideration. Some people are brilliant at sales. Terence was one of them. He knew his product inside out and only sold systems he thought were suitable for his customers (as opposed to selling something would give him the highest commission). He was already gaining a reputation as somebody to trust.

Being a good salesperson can be very financially rewarding, and some people do it all their lives, but Terence didn't want to be a sales representative for the rest of his life. Terence had dreams of selling his own products.

Advantages and Disadvantages of Selling for Other People

It is one of the easiest ways to get into your own business. It requires very little financial outlay, and if you choose the right products to white label or act as a representative for, you can earn a ton of commissions. Terence's biggest sale earned him $30,000.

You need to know your market; you need to know who the ideal client or customer would be. Also, you need to be an absolute expert at the product itself. You must know as much about the product as if you had made it yourself. This was not a problem for Terence, but if you're thinking of this route, make sure you know everything you need to know.

A disadvantage is that while the commission can be high, it's nowhere near as high as if you made the product yourself. The 20% or 30% or whatever figure you end up getting from your sales can be doubled, even trebled, if you're selling your own products,

How to Get into It

You've already made a spreadsheet of low-hanging fruit. Scrutinize this list for opportunities. If you spot an opportunity to sell other peoples' products, then contact the product or service provider.

Call or email them and tell them about yourself. Your aim on this call is to find out whether they white label products and who sells them for them. Also, to establish whether they are receptive to an agent selling their products. If they're interested, they will let you know, and at this stage, you can then talk about commission rates, etc. Also, find out what support or training they offer you to help you sell their products.

SELLING FOR YOURSELF

This would suit an individual who has no problem in sourcing his or her own products or services and creating a business around a brand designed to sell them. They'll usually be in the vanguard of selling themselves and their services/products, and all their marketing and social media, literature, will reflect this focus. For these individuals, it's not just the product, it's the brand.

Advantages and Disadvantages of Selling for Yourself

This is potentially the most profitable path to take, primarily because you make all the profit available from your products and services. You don't have to pay big clumps of commission to other people, for one thing. Plus, if you have your own products or services to sell, you're completely free to sell, however, wherever, whenever, and to whomever, you can.

If you're starting a brand or a service from scratch, you'll need more of a starting income to get it going. Interestingly, this is where most Millennial first-time entrepreneurs see themselves. Though greater rewards are in the long run, it's going to require more funding in the short run. There are ways to get around this, which we'll talk about in the finances section of this book.

Additional costs to selling for yourself include:

Your own website. You don't necessarily need this if you're selling for others. If you want a website, you'll have to fund it, and if you don't have the skills to create it yourself, you'll have to pay someone for skillset or learn it yourself. It's time-consuming but manageable. There are companies like WordPress and GoDaddy who provide a framework for your website, which means you won't have to develop any software yourself, at least not to start with, and you can customize your websites to suit your business model.

A company infrastructure. This is not as grandiose as it sounds, but you'll need to make sure every aspect of your business is covered from start to finish. You may need staff, which adds to costs and takes a bite out of profit margins. All costs do.

Harder work to get new customers. You're the new kid on the block. But a little hard work never hurt anybody. Provided you've got something meaningful to sell, which will help customers with a particular problem, you'll get there with effort.

The best way to do this is to have a clear idea of what you offer. What exactly do customers get when they pay? If you have different products or bundles to offer, be clear about what's included with the product, service, or bundle. Make sure your delivery services are crystal clear as well. This applies to any niche you're in.

REMOTE SALES (OR SELLING WITHOUT SPEAKING TO OTHERS)

The person who this kind of business might appeal to is one who doesn't necessarily want to spend most of their time talking to clients or customers to build their business. There are ways and means of doing this without having to spend all your time talking to prospective or existing clients, such as affiliate marketing, dropshipping, or blocking.

As already mentioned with affiliate marketing, you would sell other peoples' products or services (usually online), allow them to place adverts on your website, or just talk them up. If you generate web traffic to your affiliate partners site, or in some cases, generate sales, you will get paid an agreed amount, but it's the affiliate partner who deals with the fulfillment and handles all communication with their customers.

Another example might be to sell digital products or services, online training courses, or e-books. Because everything is done online, there is little to no contact with the end-users of the products.

Advantages and Disadvantages of Remote Sales

You're not limited by how many people you can speak to or network with. Particularly with digital products, there is a wide marketing world out there. You could potentially reach thousands, if not tens or hundreds of thousands of potential customers.

Digital products require work to put together but are relatively low cost if you've got the skills yourself to do it. And with dropshipping, you will present a range of products for people to buy, but the products are held elsewhere and delivered by a third-party. The only initial costs you incur are the setting up of your website and marketing activities. You could operate a business similar to Amazon (but on a massively smaller scale) without having the headache of tying up your funds in stock or worrying about where to keep the stock.

You need to have a very strong online presence because this is where your sales are going to come from. This can take a lot of work and, if you go the advertising or marketing route, it can be quite expensive. On the dropshipping side, margins are very low. You need to sell a lot before getting a decent return. Also, you will still need to set yourself up to deal with faulty products or customer complaints. Dropshipping companies won't do that for you.

It also requires you to have some technical knowledge to build a great website, and if not, you have to hire the skill.

You will also need knowledge of online advertising and an understanding of how much you can afford to spend on advertising to acquire new customers, while at the same time leaving enough for you to make a living from it.

Plus, if you've gone into this kind of business because you don't like talking to other people, I'm sorry to disappoint you, but you will still need some interaction with a variety of people, including your affiliate partners, the dropshipping companies you strike agreements with, and customers who buy your online training courses for instance.

To grow your business, you will still need to network and still need people working for you if you get big enough. However, if you're not sold on the direct selling aspect of other business models, this one might be for you. There are plenty of successful people out there who make money from drop shipping or affiliate marketing, but this is the one you will need more readily available funds for.

THE COMBO

Of course, you don't have to follow these guidelines rigidly. You're the best person to know what type of business will suit your personality. And, there's no reason you couldn't blend all three types of businesses in some form or other. Sell other peoples' products, sell your own products, and indulge in a little bit of affiliate marketing at the same time. You don't have to do all three, you could take a couple of these elements and blend them together according to the needs of your business.

A great example is Amazon. Amazon sells a phenomenal amount of product. Recent estimates put their total product range at 353 million. But here's the kicker Amazon offers vendors a service called Marketplace. It's a form of dropshipping where the vendor sends their goods to an Amazon warehouse, and Amazon presents them on their website and delivers them as if they are Amazon products. This comprises 341 million of their entire range of products! The other 12 million are sourced and supplied by Amazon themselves. Here you have a hugely successful business that combines the notion of selling other peoples' products and selling their own.

Terence's Big Idea

Our friend Terence has an idea, which is where his business is going. He wants to develop his own integrated telephony system. A system that will deal with voice calls, inquiries via the Internet, demand from social media, and online demand. It'll handle everything.

His ambition is to design his own hardware and create and patent his own software. The hardware itself is the easiest part, though still complex enough. It's the integrated software he's in the process of developing that he believes gives him an edge.

Currently, he's still selling white-label products, still acting as a representative for other telephony companies, but his ultimate goal is to eventually have his own product, created, maintained, branded, and sold by his own company. He is under no illusions of the work this will take, not just in the software development, the most complex part of all, but also the creation of his own brand, website, media marketing, presence, etc. That's where he sees himself in 3 to 5 years.

The point here is this. Maybe you see yourself in a similar position to Terence, where you have some great ideas for your own products but currently don't have the resources to develop them. There's absolutely nothing wrong with starting a type of business that doesn't necessarily fit your personality or where you want to be.

It could form part of an overarching scheme to move in the direction you want to go, which in Terence's case is sourcing and selling his own products.

Mixing and matching businesses require different types of personalities. That may not just be a good thing to do, it may be the only thing for you to do to realize your own specific ambitions.

I spent a lot of time on SEO, I knew it wasn't where I wanted to be, but it served its purpose. It helped fund me and my business to move into areas that are more enjoyable and profitable.

Feel free to review the three types of personalities and match your own, but also take a hard-nosed look at your own situation. If you do something you don't want to do to get to where you want to be, there's nothing wrong with this path. I've already mentioned how Terence decided, rather than give up the useful income stream of repairing computers which she had grown to personally hate doing himself, he outsourced it. He barely learned to cope with this particular aspect of his business, and it is to his credit he made a significant and important change.

He tried several different people before landing on a couple of individuals whose work he was very satisfied with. He learned by doing. He practiced his entrepreneurial skill of keeping part of the business going while letting go and delegating the part he didn't like. He had to practice assessing and reviewing the performance of other people, collecting payments owed, and ensuring his outsourced staff received payment, too. This required more knowledge and control over his budgets and finances than he was used to. Practice, practice, practice. Mistakes were made, but he got there through practice, patience, and persistence.

We'll take an in-depth look at these three personality types in the next section.

FINDING A BUSINESS
THAT SUITS YOUR PERSONALITY –
PART 2: SALES MODELS

When I first started in my own business, I loved the idea of selling without necessarily having much contact with people, simply because the concept of recommending somebody else's products via affiliate marketing and being paid for it sounded like the easiest path to making lots of money. I know better now.

I know that to be able to sell and make money like that can potentially be the most expensive route to market of all because you need to have a community of people to sell to. You need access to a large list of followers, via email or social media, who will listen to what you have to say and be interested in the product or service you offer.

Building this list is time-consuming and, from a marketing perspective, expensive. When I first started this book, I wanted to show you a way to make money without initially having a lot of money to spend. I'm going to suggest a pathway to you, using all three business types which will involve you amassing the kind of following you need, and getting a chunk of funds behind you. Moving into selling without talking to people becomes almost seamless.

I still love the affiliate marketing model. I think in the future, it's something I intend to get more involved with. But it's all about the funding. The first part of the path, selling other people's things, is the one that requires the least outlay on your part. The second part, selling your own things, does require some outlay, not as much as the third aspect, but still some. But selling your own products/services should mean your profits are larger too, and you've been paving the way by selling other people's stuff. The third and last part of the path is selling without talking to people. The work you do paves the way for this method.

This path, using all three personalities, is only a suggestion. You may find yourself selling other peoples' products, enjoying it, and making as much money as you want, and that's maybe where you stop. If you like it and you're making enough money, go for it. That goes for selling your own products, too. You may be entirely happy there.

On the other hand, you may want to get straight into the affiliate marketing side, or other business models, which means you can make money without too much contact with the people who buy your products or services. It's the route that requires the most financial outlay to start.

If that's what you have your heart set on, go for it. In this section, we'll talk about how to reach the third stage incrementally, so you don't have to break the bank to get started (and I keep my promise to you). In the process, I'll be giving you more detail about each of the three business types with some examples. In summary, the path is this:

Stage One. Sell other peoples' products and services. Make enough money and build enough of a reputation to jump onto stage two.

Stage Two. Sell your own products or services. Increase your profit margins, make more money, and increase your reputation, your email list, and a tribe of followers. Then, you can comfortably jump onto stage three.

Stage Three. Sell without speaking to customers. Keep doing it, using your email list and social media followers. This is often called your online community. From now on, if I refer to "community", it's this tribe of followers.

The art of selling

There's a very real chance some of you going into business are going to be involved in some face-to-face or telephone selling. I would argue that, in all three business types, you need to be selling. In every transaction you have with somebody you need to be selling.

Selling has a particular connotation that can put people off. If you've ever seen the film Glengarry Glen Ross, the real estate salesmen in are some of the unpleasant and narcissistic people you have ever met. All they care about is making money. The main character is a desperately troubled concocter of stories who lies to his customers with almost every word he says and turns out to be a thief as well.

Think of Gil in The Simpsons, another desperate character who begs you to buy his products; otherwise, he's going to get fired. Many media images portray salesmen as either desperate or unscrupulous. Perhaps there are people out there like that, but in reality, nothing could be further from the truth. Good salespeople care about the products and care about the people they're selling to. Here is a list of qualities good salespeople have.

Great listeners. You can't establish a customer's needs without good listening skills. Most great salespeople, when face-to-face with clients, spend more time listening than talking to clients. A great listener is usually attuned to all the words a prospect is saying, whether verbal or written.

Empathy. Good salespeople are to relate to their customers' needs and get behind those needs to discover the real emotions behind their customers' buying motives. You can't do this without having empathy for your clients.

Honesty. This is where the Glengarry Glen Ross analogy falls apart. The best salespeople are also the most honest. They know one shady word or incorrect piece of information could destroy a deal. In most businesses, you want to attract repeat customers. You may get away with dishonest dealings once, but never again.

Enthusiasm and passion. Unlike Gil from The Simpsons, you have to be enthusiastic about your product, enthusiastic about life, and enthusiastic about the customer's needs.

Persistence, patience, and tenacity. Good salespeople know how to get the job done. Trying to speak to a buyer can be a dogged task and usually requires a salesperson ignores being told "no" and keeps trying to get his/her foot in the door on at least three occasions, possibly more. This isn't rudeness; it just means the salesperson will have a process to make a specific number of attempts at contact with the buyer before moving on.

Attention to detail and thoroughness. You need to know what you're selling but also know what your customer's needs are and write down and act upon what you promised them. Customers love it when you do this.

Understanding the value beyond the cost. Buying something isn't just all about the price a customer pays for a product. The value of a product or service you provide will be in what it can do for your customers. Good salespeople are aware of this.

Great communication. To be good at selling, you need to be a great communicator, both face-to-face and in writing. You need to be able to paraphrase what the customer is saying, avoid jargon, and get to the point of the customer's needs.

This is by no means a definitive list, but it covers the most important points. Let me tell you the qualities make a bad salesman. Dishonesty, aggression, inability to listen, more interested in making commission than assessing the needs of their customers, grumpiness, sadness, desperation. The clichés demonstrated in Glengarry Glen Ross or The Simpsons are for people who shouldn't be salespeople.

You may not feel like a natural salesperson, but selling can be learned. If you're a genuine person who wants to help people by selling them products or services that meet their needs, you'll soon learn. Or you'll have skinny kids. (Not my punchline. That's Zig Ziglar.)

The science of selling

There is a principle behind selling that may help you. It's the process of getting yourself known to a prospect and getting to the point where you close the deal. It's called A.I.D.A, which is an acronym for Attention or awareness, Interest, Desire, and Action.

Attention. The prospective customer is made aware of or becomes aware of particular products or services he or she might be interested in.

Interest. The prospective customer becomes interested in learning more about the products or services and how they could benefit him or her.

Desire. The prospective customer views the products or services positively.

Action. The prospective customer buys the product or takes an action that gets them nearer to buying it.

This is a useful model from which you could hang all of your sales strategies. For instance, if you were having a face-to-face meeting. You would be grabbing the **attention** of the prospect; you'll be holding their attention through making the customer **interested** in the product itself; then you will be arousing a **desire** to buy by creating confidence and belief in the product; and finally, in the closing part, you will be securing the decision and taking **action**, creating satisfaction.

It's straightforward and helps, but life isn't always like that. Here's an example.

Terence went to a seminar hosted by a local call center, which he'd heard was having telephony issues. He introduced himself to the decision-maker, the CEO of the company. He said, "My name is Terence, and I help call centers achieve world-class customer service."

He immediately had the attention of the CEO. He continued, "I do this by catering to the needs of all contact centers with telephone solutions help solve customer issues quickly, not make them worse."

At this stage, he continued to hold the attention and the interest of the CEO, and then he stopped short and asked the CEO a question. He asked, "How quickly does your current call center answer the phone?"

He knew this had been a problem. He'd read somewhere customers had been on hold for up to 30-40 minutes and not been answered.

Terence's question (according to Terence) jolted the CEO. "It could be better," he replied.

Terence said, "It would be great to speak to you about improving those service levels by integrating all your inquiries at a relatively low-cost." At this stage, the CEO didn't say anything but still seemed interested, so Terence took a gamble and went into his close. Remember, the point of this conversation wasn't to sell the customer a telephony system there and then, but to secure an appointment with him.

Terence said, "I'd love to chat with you about your current situation and your needs for half an hour or so because I think I could offer you an ideal solution. Could we set something up?" This was a close, not a very elegant one, but Terence asked for the call, and the only answer he was likely to get was yes or no.

"Yes," said the CEO, "that will be fine. Here is my card give me a call on Monday." Bingo. Terence got what he wanted. But, he didn't have very long to talk to the customer.

Even in that short span, what he did worked well for him. He got the CEO's attention by speaking to him about his business, about an issue that was bothering the CEO, and asking a brilliantly timed question. It was AIDA in action.

He created a desire by talking very briefly about a solution before transitioning into his close. He got the appointment. About four meetings later, he closed the entire deal.

Selling takes all forms. The AIDA model doesn't just work in verbal communication like face-to-face meetings. It also works in written communication like emails and sales letters. If your email is an attempt to get a telephone conversation going, it could be worded like this:

- After our conversation at the conference, I like the way you do X – Attention

- I've thought of a way you could do it for half the price – Interest

- You could increase profit by saving 50% of the cost – Desire

- Here is a list of clients who have increased their profit thanks to our product – Desire

- It would be great to have a brief conversation over the phone. Are you available? If not, let me know when you are. – Action

Again, this is just a brief example, I'm sure you could come up with your own. The most important part is Action. Close, always close, whether it be asking for an appointment or for the sale.

There are lots of sales technique books out there, most of them are extremely disingenuous and manipulative. The core is this. Does the customer have a particular issue or problem? Or could he benefit from making more money?

If the answer to either of those two questions is yes (and who would say no to the second question?), then the next question is – do you have something that could help solve the customer's problem or make him or her more money? If the answer to the question is a genuine yes, then you can approach the customer from the stance of integrity and sincerity. Anything you do to help get yourself the appointment or the sale is not just helping you, it's helping your customer. Keep that in mind.

The essence of the above is that selling is not a dirty word, and you should get used to it.

A DEEP DIVE INTO THE SALES MODELS

Selling for others

From the call center telephony side, Terence is selling for others. It's also how I started with search engine optimization. I did it for other people before doing it for myself. Let's take a closer look at exactly what white labeling is all about. If you recall, white labeling is a form of selling for others.

White labeling. We need to distinguish between white labeling for products, such as Terence's model is telephony systems, and white labeling for services, such as my search engine optimization business.

Overall, white label items are manufactured or created by a particular vendor or supplier, rebranded, and sold to a customer. The advantage to the supplier is that, through their white label affiliates, they sell more of their supplies, and it allows their affiliates to expand their own product line, sell them, and make money without having to make the products.

I've already mentioned it once. Just have a look at the self-label breakfast cereals in your local superstore. Or the cookies or washing powder. You will see tons of own-label products made by other people. It's a huge business for products and services. A few services that could be white-labelled are web design, SEO, digital branding, online advertising, software development, and even recruitment.

Sometimes white label is called private label. These terms are used interchangeably, particularly when talking about the rebranding of software and services. There is also co-branding. I only mention this because sometimes white labeling gets confused with this. Co-branding is when the original supplier's brand is added to the products as well as the reseller's brand. This is something very different, and not something we will get into now.

There is also a difference between white labeling and outsourcing. With outsourcing, a company pays somebody to complete a function of their business, but essentially, it's still branded as the originator's product. If you wanted to outsource your marketing, it would still be under your name.

White labeling is very similar to an affiliate program; the big difference being you get to sell these products face-to-face.

Why white-label? If you're a vendor or supplier who wants to white label, you get to expand your offerings to a wider market. You could potentially land bigger clients because you can offer more products and services, even if the products are not branded as yours. Do you want to improve and enhance your company's brand? If so, white labeling might not be for you. Or do you want to expand market share, volume, and sales and are not too worried about brand awareness? White labeling might be for you.

The advantages to you as an entrepreneur if you sell white-label products:

- You get involved in a much wider market, with a bigger and possibly better product, if you choose your partners well.

- You get to make good commission.

- You get to learn all about the products and the business you're in for a small cost, vital if you want to jump to stage two (selling for yourself) at some stage.

Plus, you can white-label other peoples' products or services, or you can do what Terence did.

Act as an agent for other peoples' products. Instead of white labeling products, you're selling the products as they are. You're not working directly for the company whose products you sell but are acting as an agent for them.

Compared to white labeling, the rewards are similar, and the learning curve is much the same. The big difference is you're selling products under their own brand name, and if the brand name is popular, you could potentially sell a lot more. In many ways, if you're acting as an agent for a well-known brand, it makes your life easier. The key thing is, be passionate, enthusiastic, and knowledgeable about the product or services you're selling.

If you get into something you're passionate about, you'll impress your potential partners because they need to be comfortable. The person selling their products and services is professional and efficient too. The more experience you have, the more you can talk fluently about the products/services. It will put you in good standing for when you make a move to stage two of the path, selling for yourself.

My business revolves around Facebook ads, and it's grown into a pretty big beast. If you're reading this as somebody who loves Facebook ads but is still in a learning curve.

You might look at my business, read my reviews, check out my testaments and social proof, and be interested. Maybe you'll approach me and offer to sell my services for a fee.

I check you out, we have a talk, and we agree on something. Either we agree, you will sell my services under a white label arrangement, or you just sell my services for a commission. I get the advantage of having somebody bright and enthusiastic selling my services in places I'm currently not.

What you get is to piggyback on my experience, my reputation, my resources, my case studies, and social proof, my branding even - but you also get to learn as much as you can in the process about every single aspect of the business. It's a win-win situation. I use this as a hypothetical situation.

This is exactly what Terence has been doing with his telephony systems, learning all about the way they work, the pricing structure, the margins, the technology, and because he's doing a fine job, he's making a fine dollar out of the whole process.

When you sell somebody else's products in the way Terence does, you essentially act as if you're an intrinsic part of the company, the products, their development, etc. This is not deceitful because, for all intents and purposes, you're a part of the company while you're selling their products. It's how you present it.

If Terence goes into a presentation, finds out what a prospect's telephony requirements are, then says something like, "Of the 8 to 10 systems I act on behalf of, here is the one or two I would recommend to you."

There's nothing inherently wrong with this approach, but right then, from the prospect's perspective, Terence is another sales guy, an agent. He's virtually said so.

Imagine if Terence says, "From what you've told me, you need x, y, and z, and I have a system I could show you that matches your needs. Here it is." Or even, "I have two systems that will be perfect for you, one is for 100 agents, which is where you're at now, and one is for up to 500 agents, which is where you'd like to be." How different does it sound? It's not deceitful; it's Terence demonstrating ownership of the entire process, and great selling ability too.

By selling other peoples' products, whether white-label or as an agent, you're learning a ton of information about the products, the market, and your business. If you start by selling your own products, you would be learning this from scratch.

Everything you learn is going to help you in the long run. Everything. You'll be able to try different sales approaches, and you'll be handling your finances

While you're about it, you'll keep making those contacts and keep building up your network. Start by creating an email list of people who might be interested in what you do. This list will be vital for your future success, whatever business model you end up staying in.

The other thing about this approach is the funding aspect. It's low-cost, almost no-cost in some cases, and if you do it well, you could make a lot of money – money you could put away for the day you want to sell your own products or services.

In addition to everything you're learning, you're getting more and more ready to do it yourself, whatever it is you're selling for other people.

When I went into search engine optimization, after learning how to do it well, I started by white labeling for other people. I was doing all the initial work. The company I was white labeling took care of the rest.

As I was doing it, I was learning more and more about the business, and it got to the point where I was able to do everything the white labeling company was doing.

That's when I made a move. Instead of selling the service, I sold and provided the service. From the client's perspective, nothing had changed. It was smooth. That's important. It's what you want to aim for, a smooth transition period.

Selling for Yourself

You might be reading this section and want to go straight into selling your own thing. Maybe you've got a product, concept, or service that doesn't take a huge amount of investment. For instance, with search engine optimization, you're generally able to do it (provided you know what you're doing) without having to buy anything additional.

But to be able to do well and to be able to make money, you have to build up a reputation. You have to build up your skillset, a lot of which you learn on the go, about staffing, finances, legal requirements, and all the

But if you follow the path I'm recommending, you can go from earning money by selling for other people straight onto earning money through something for yourself. The secret is, as I've already said, to make the transition as seamless as possible. Of course, just how seamless depends on the type of business you're in. For my SEO business, I was able to make it straightforward, with almost no hitch.

For Terence and his telephony systems, it's a much longer-term plan, but still, he intends to make it as unified as possible.

For my SEO or my Facebook ads, we're talking about a tangible service was being provided. The fruits of my labor, the way a website looks, the wording, the content, can be seen by all, but it's an easy thing to transition from one business owner to another. One minute, I was talking to one of my clients, and the work was being done elsewhere. The next week, I was talking to the same client, and I was doing all the work myself.

But for Terence, the smoothness of transition will all be in the relationships he has forged and the reputation he has built. When people talk to Terence, they trust him. With a brand-new product developed by himself, if he had not earned and cultivated trust, contacting prospective new clients would be a lot tougher.

Terence is the guy they trust. So, if he talks about something new, they're going to listen. He's learned a number of these previous customers are going to be moving offices or changing telephone systems in the next 2 to 5 years. And this fits in beautifully with his plan. The transition won't be product-specific. It will be about keeping in touch with his client base and then segueing into talking about his own product.

In summary, Terence's relationships will be priceless, and this will get his foot in the door of prospective new clients much more quickly than if he was calling from a cold start.

What I cannot emphasize enough is while you're selling other peoples' products, you still need to work hard at forging productive relationships and building up your community. You should be enriching your network at all times, and if you work it properly, you'll enhance your reputation. We'll talk specifically about how to do it in the next chapter. The bigger your email list, the bigger your community, the easier it will be to get into selling without talking to people. Let's get into it.

Selling Without Talking to People

There are many avenues open to you when selling without talking to people. I'm going to dwell just a few. I've already mentioned affiliate marketing; I genuinely think it's the most lucrative approach. We'll discuss that in more detail.

There are other methods, such as dropshipping, some forms of e-commerce, and even blogging, or a combination of all of them.

This is why I have said there is no particular reason why you can't mix-and-match what suits your business, at least to start with. I'm interested in affiliate marketing, but not as a replacement to my current businesses, more as a compliment.

A Closer Look at Affiliate Marketing. If you have gone through this book, you already know affiliate marketing is when you allow or have a deal with a separate business partner to advertise or push or mention their services or products. Usually, you provide a link to their website or a link to their particular buying page. Some affiliate agreements involve getting traffic to somebody's site, and some of them involve you getting the customers to buy a product – that's how you get paid. The big questions are: What is it you're demonstrating? What is it you're showing? How do people see these adverts?

Who is involved in the affiliate program? First, you need to find a merchant. The merchant is also known as the manufacturer, or creator, sometimes even the retailer or vendor. This is the party that creates the products or services.

Some huge merchants indulge in affiliate marketing and some small ones too. Then there is the affiliate, that's you. An affiliate could be a single individual or a large company. To start with, you might end up earning a few hundred dollars in commission, and the aim is to grow as much as you possibly can, which is where marketing comes in.

Affiliate vendors are much more interested in those companies or people who have a ready-made bank of people to market to. That's why trying to get into affiliate marketing from a cold start is difficult. You have nobody to talk to when you first start. Nobody knows you. It's the coldest of cold starts. In order, therefore, to get people to talk to you, you would have to do a huge amount of marketing, and it can be pretty expensive.

That is why I have been beating the drum about building up your network, building up your followers, building up your own community at whatever stage you are, whether selling for other people or yourself.

The more successful you have been in building up this bank of followers, then the greater your chances of being a successful affiliate marketer. The more traffic you have to your own website, the more attractive you will be to potential partners. We are going to talk about building up followers and forging relationships in the next chapter.

Imagine having an email list of 10,000 people and a great reputation in your marketplace. You email your 10,000-strong community. You tell them that you've found a product you want to recommend. Let's say 7,000 are into it, and 2,000 purchase. You make $50 per transaction. Boom. You've just made $100,000 for very little work. Imagine doing that every two months, even more from a larger following.

That is the Nirvana of affiliate marketing. But first, you have to have a reputation, and you have to have an active list of people who listen to you. There are two important things to remember about affiliate products:

1. Don't get into an affiliate agreement with a product or services that have nothing to do with your core business.
2. Don't recommend something unless you're sure it's a high-quality product or service.

Imagine having this bank of people who trust you. You persuade them to buy a particular product, and it turns out to be either nothing to do with your core business or completely trash, breaking down as soon as customers have used it. That's a surefire way of tarnishing your own reputation. Recommend products that match your reputation, are high quality, and reliable.

Finding an Affiliate Program That Suits You. There are lots of sources out there. These three are considered the best: Clickbank, JV Zoo, and CJ Affiliate. Don't take my word for it, go on the hunt yourself.

I will stress once more how important it is to find programs, services, and products that match your company's brand or brands, your reputation, and your standing in the market. Don't try and sell something irrelevant to you (for instance, if Terence tried to sell shoes on his website promoting telephony solutions, it would be strange and surreal – it would look like a mistake) and don't promote anything that is poor quality. It will come back and bite you.

Another Way to Sell Without Talking to People

There are tens of thousands of blogs out there, covering tens of thousands of subjects. What I want to concentrate on here is those blogs are used to complement your business. I don't want to dwell too much on it, but a regularly written blog, i.e., at least once a week, which hones in on solving the problems of your prospective customers is a surefire way of helping increase your email list and, provided the SEO is efficient, can be a brilliant way of getting your website and its products up the search ladder.

While we're talking about blogging, the same thing applies to video blogs on YouTube or even Podcasts, something I've been getting into more and more.

They can all be embedded into the same page on your website, and they can complement each other. Your blog could be the same subject as your YouTube entry for the week.

All of these things enhance your reputation, increase your profile, and potentially give you more and more opportunities for affiliate marketing. It takes effort, but you need to investigate whether it's worth making an effort, I personally think it is. If you take the blogging route, here are some tips:

- Post regularly.

- Make the information you post pertinent to your customers and make the information useful.

- Switch on the comment section. Ask for comments. This is a great way of spotting potential new prospects as well as getting feedback on your entire business.

- Make it very easy for people to subscribe to your blog.

- Share what you write on other platforms, particularly social media.

- If you're blogging, vlogging, and/or podcasting, make sure they're all about the same thing.

- Make it easy to read. Use bullet points, numbers, or other formatting techniques that allow your customers to focus on the information that's most important to them.

- Proofread it ruthlessly. Don't produce blogs that are either poorly written or written with grammar or punctuation errors. They distract potential customers and look unprofessional. If you need, get someone to read it for you.

- Don't just make it about your business, make it about you as well. Let people see a little bit of you in business. Share relevant anecdotes. Don't be afraid to let people know about other aspects of your life (like your family – I put a condition on this. Don't reveal sensitive information). All of these things humanize you, and people buy from people.

To build up momentum with a blog, to amass a bank of loyal readers to add to your network and community, be patient, and persistent. When it comes to blogging, the tortoise always wins, not the hare.

There are several other ways to compound your sales models without talking to people. One way that I have created a lot of success for my clients is through automated systems. This is where my online expertise shines. You can create an ad that leads to a sales page that processes your order and delivers your products. You know a sale's been made when you hear your phone ding, and a message pops on your screen, "Payment of…"

Ultimately, you have to ask yourself which avenue of business is best for you. It could be one avenue; it could be several.

Checking in on Terence

Terence has a clear idea of what his main path is going to be. He didn't always have, one and that's why choosing several avenues to start his business helped him. At this stage, the bulk of his revenue comes from selling for other people with his telephony systems, but he has made a successful go of providing PA systems and also computer repair.

Both strands of his business took a path he wasn't expecting. He knew he was going to DJ once in a while, but this rarely happens. He has half a dozen PA kits that people can hire for DJing or just for public address systems. Most of the equipment is hired out three or four times a week nowadays. He also has a bank of reputable presenters and DJs who he has checked himself. They either hire his kit out, or he will put them on to a job, for which he will take a small cut.

As far as the computer repair side of things, he was set to give up almost as soon as he could. He contracts out most of the repairs. He takes the order. Somebody else does the repair. Terence gets 40% of the revenue, the repairer 60%.

It's not a bad deal for either of them. He's still repairing 15 to 20 items a week with an average value of $90. There are marketing costs, but it's still worth it.

He has successfully compartmentalized elements of his business. He's spending less time on them, yet making just as much, and sometimes more, money.

This allows him to concentrate on the lion's share of his activity on telephony and eventually making his own telephone system. He is less interested in affiliate marketing at this stage, but that's only a time thing. He tells me he is interested in looking at it at a later stage when he's built a bigger client base. Because he loves writing, he's going to start a blog on telephony, and he is very excited to see how it goes.

It's time to move to step four of your successful business, which is all about forging productive relationships.

CHAPTER 4

Step Four – Forging Productive Relationships

I cannot overstate how important it is to every aspect of your business that you create fruitful relationships. It goes without saying you have to create good relationships with your clients, especially if you want repeat business. Also, your clients will be banging the drum for you if you do a good job for them. Statistics show that, for every good experience a client has, they will tell four people, but for every bad experience, they will tell nine.

You also must forge productive relationships with the people you outsourced to, your affiliate marketers, or your employees (naturally). Truthfully, it's in your best interest to develop productive relationships with just about anybody you come into contact with that is not a detriment to you and the goals you set in the first step.

But what I want to dwell on is the forging of productive relationships will help your business and you, personally, grow. Ultimately, the speed of your success and your success overall will largely depend on how successful you're at interacting with the people around you. I'll explain more.

Social media and Millennials

Millennials and post-Millennials live in the age of Facebook. Yes, I know there are a lot more social network sites out there, but with its number of users at over 2 billion, Facebook is by far the biggest social network on the planet. To be more accurate, we should say we live in the age of social networking, where it becomes much easier to contact like-minded people.

Of course, there are issues with social media, such as fake accounts, fake news, online bullying, social isolation, etc. But for me and most people my age, by far the most popular way of staying in touch with friends and getting in touch with old friends or people who interest you is Facebook.

My point is Millennials trying to go into business have a fantastic advantage in being able to exploit the vast arena of information on social media by expanding friendships and connecting with like-minded individuals, either from a personal or business perspective. The business perspective is what we're looking at.

I'm going to give you a step-by-step process to create and maintain a network of contacts that will not only be the envy of anybody in your business but will help your business grow and keep growing.

CREATING AND MAINTAINING A FANTASTIC NETWORK

The foundations of this method are as follows:

1. Always work hard to grow your network.

2. Don't think of your network as just people who you can get business from.

3. Of course, you will get business from some of them, but rather, think of your network as a large group of people who you can help and who can help you in return. In this instance, the reciprocation is the currency.

4. Think of what you need to know, and what help you need to grow your business. Then, tailor your network to being around people who can help you grow.

5. Don't just make friends or contacts that are at the same level as you, not if you want to grow your business and learn new things.

6. Building a robust network is a long-term task. Keep at it.

Step 1 – Analyze and trim your current network

Facebook (or social networks in general) is a great place to start. Have a close look at all your friends, see if any of those people belong in your desired network. You're looking to forge closer business relationships. This does not necessarily mean these people are going to give your business (though some might, you never know), but they may be able to help you improve an aspect of your business, and you may be able to reciprocate.

Start looking through their friend's lists to establish contact with other potential contacts. Facebook is an easy way. Plus, search for groups in the relevant areas. You could search for recruiters, salesman, software developers, management groups, and specialists in your relevant field. Anybody and everybody who you think might be a useful person to know now and in the future. Anybody who can help grow your business, either through becoming a client or providing education in some form for you.

Here's the other thing. Facebook is a great place for making and staying in touch with friends all over the globe. If you use it for that, as I still do, excellent. But you almost have to think of your Facebook profile as being a window for everybody to see what you're about, including, no, especially the business side of your life.

The biggest bank of Facebook and other social media friends should be all about the business side of things. You don't want the bulk of these to be people on the same level as you and/or doing what you do. Otherwise, how are you going to learn anything new? How are you going to get exposure to the movers and shakers of this world, the people whose businesses are as big as you want yours to be?

I apply an old rule here, one that's been used in several different scenarios over the years, and that's the 80/20 rule. I want 80% of my social media friends to be aspirational for me because they are people who, in some way, can help me take some aspect of my business to another level, and I want the rest to be my business buddies, my gossip partners, the people who are going through the same old stuff I am, and who wouldn't be the first people I'd look to for my own business growth.

The secret is to connect with people in your industry who have something different to offer. Hopefully, you 'll have something unique to offer them to will help their business grow.

Let me offer two examples. You know if you expand your business, you're going to have to take on more and more staff. You're going to need to learn about recruitment. You're interested in building great teams, and you may be interested in people who have expanded quickly and had to do everything speedily.

I mention this because when a company does things quickly, it tends to make more mistakes as they're learning at such a rapid pace. Not only do you learn from your own mistakes, but also from the mistakes of other people. These are the people you should keep a special eye out for when expanding your network.

The second example is real estate. I've always been fascinated with real estate. It's the kind of area I'd like to get into later in life. Real estate is one of my aspirations. To make big money from real estate, you need access to big cash. If you do it well, you could make a lot of money for little effort. (I make an extra effort to involve good real estate people in my network.)

In summary, make a list of areas of your business and life that will help you expand your business and earnings. Include in this list people who will help you learn. Of course, including potential new customers!

Look at people who are earning 10 times more than you or even more. Perhaps your aspirational annual profit is $10 million. Look at businesses that are scaled to that size as well. You want to grow, you want to learn, and it's best to grow and learn from people who have already done it.

Step 2 – Cultivate and nurture the relationships

Cultivating is such a lovely word, bringing up images of growing in a garden by nurturing the plants and flowers. It's a nice metaphor for your network. You're the gardener enriching the relationships you have, so you both grow. Everybody wins.

The big question you should have on your mind when interacting with people on your network is – how can we help each other?

Because what you need to start doing is talking to these people, either face-to-face or usually via email, messenger, or text. Based on the plan we've been working on, your ultimate goal is to expand your business and to get new business regularly, which means you should always be on the lookout for new business – keep it front and center of your mind.

When you contact somebody who you think can show you something you need, for example, the ability to grow your team, consider what it is you need to know. Write down some questions:

How many clients can I handle myself before needing help?

How many additional clients do I need to make an extra member of staff worthwhile?

How many additional clients do I need to take on two, three, four, and more staff?

What are the pay-rates for my business and the positions I could be hiring for?

There are loads of questions to ask when expanding your staff and creating teams, and what you're looking for in your network is a couple of people who can help you answer these questions.

Contact people who have been through these experiences in your network and ask them if they can provide insight on how they grew from, say, one person to 10 people, or point you in the direction of somebody who can help.

Most people love helping people. If all your conversations or messages are respectful and highlight what you like about the person's business who you're asking for help, they will probably help you.

An example message, "Hi Dave, I notice five years ago you were a one-man-band. I think it's incredible the way you've gone from having one team member to 30 people on your staff. I'd love to gain some insight into how you did that, or if you have any tips on where I can go to get information."

Get the conversation started. If you do this right, your contact is going to respond in one of two ways. First, he is going to offer you some help. He may give you the information himself helps you.

Second, he might say he's not the best person to talk to, or he is not able to help you with your particular issue, but he will point you in the direction of somebody on his list of contacts who will help you. What you're doing is expanding your network as well by having this new person as a contact. Either way, you win.

Step 3 – Reciprocation

After you've had all this communication, you will inevitably want to reciprocate. You can ask them, "You've been very helpful. How can I help or support you?"

it may well be what they need is some help with online advertising – which is great for me! But whatever your business area, they might need some contact details for somebody else you may have in your network list. The more your network grows, the more often this happens. If not, just tell them what you do and what you can help with. As well as talking about what you sell, this allows you to help in other ways, not just business.

Terence asks if his contact knows of anybody who is moving premises or expanding their operations in the future because that's when people usually look at new infrastructure and telephony.

What I ask is phrased something like this, "Do you or does anybody in your network need any help with advertising? I'd love to be able to help them grow their business." Notice, I

138

keep focused on the needs of the person I'm talking to, growing their business.

This is how I've bagged myself an incredible number of referrals by simply asking. But it's a process. I ask how I can help them first, and I help them if I can.

I can't remember any time when I've helped people, even if it's just with a contact, somebody else hasn't replied by thanking me and asking me if I need help from them. It's happened almost every single time.

Keep Searching

I know I spent a lot of time talking about Facebook, but that's because it's what I do naturally. It's also a great vehicle for searching in groups.

Of course, there are not just social media. The entire web is open to you via search engines like Google, Bing, Yahoo, etc. Don't forget to look at business groups on Google or groups that are native to your industry.

If you were looking for a specialist skill, type it in; you want recruitment help, type in recruitment specialists. You want help forming teams? Type in the words "team-building" and a thousand pages will come back to you.

Although I'm advocating building your network up as much as you can, you need to be mindful of quality too. You need to do a little bit of homework on the people you're placing in your network; you don't want to place anybody just to make up numbers.

There's a bit of due diligence on your part, which won't take very long. Perhaps they share a lot of posts. Lots of posts don't necessarily mean they're a successful business. That could be all they do. You need to dig deeper.

Look at the nature of the posts your prospective new contact makes, the subject matter, the way they're written, the quality of the content. Look at who else is interacting with you. If you recognize some names from your network, you know you're in the right ballpark.

Look at the quality of the interactions. Look at who else (other than from your own network) the contact is communicating with. If what you've seen impresses you, go to the next phase.

Dig into their business information. Look at their website and social media presence. Scrutinize anything on their profile that will give you more information on them. If it all sounds time-consuming, it isn't. Almost all the information I've talked about will be at your fingertips. It's worth it because the big question to ask is – **can I provide them with some value? And can they reciprocate by providing me with some value?**

In summary, when you're conducting your due diligence, look for people who are delivering insight makes you think, makes you believe you could possibly use what they've got.

Connect with them and start following them. You should be able to see even more of their content if you do this. Look for case studies, i.e., things they have done and how long it's taken them. Is there something resonates with you immediately? Good, put them on the top of your list to contact. If not, but there's something you think might be useful in the future, make a note of it.

Don't forget. People love people, and people buy from people. During this due diligence, take note of any hobbies they have, or what family surround them. You're not doing this to be stalkerish; in the end, with a diverse view of all the content available, you hope to make deep connections with these people, and the more you know about them, the easier becomes.

Leave no stone unturned, look everywhere you can. Don't forget LinkedIn, either, especially for the business side of things.

Building Networks Without the Internet

Although forging online networks is a much easier process, do not discount the ability and potential to forge relationships off the internet. The amount of people you meet is smaller than on the internet, but if you look in the right places, the quality is much higher. By quality, I mean people who match what you're looking for.

There are networking groups that meet up regularly for small businesses. See this one in your area. There are Meetup groups too, where, if you look online initially, you'll potentially find all kinds of groups who get together regularly.

All over the world, seminars, conferences, and exhibitions are happening, where, depending on the size of the event, you could get to meet dozens of like-minded people in a short period. For now, I want to focus on something called Mastermind Groups.

What are Mastermind Groups?

Mastermind groups have been around for nearly 100 years. It's just a fancy term for a group of people who meet to discuss their current goals and to see if they can help each other. It's a bit like networking on steroids. In the mastermind group, everybody is happy to share their business goals, and everybody is open to providing constructive feedback to help other people achieve those goals.

Many mastermind groups meet online through conference facilities, group chats, etc. Many meet face-to-face – it's said these are the most productive types of meetings. To find out about them, ask around in your networks and do some more digging online because a good mastermind group is invaluable. Whether you're stuck in a rut, your business has plateaued, or your enterprise is experiencing slower growth than you'd like, a good-quality mastermind group can provide fresh ideas and perspectives, accountability, resources, and an overall boost in energy required to elevate your business to new heights.

One of the reasons I love mastermind groups, especially face-to-face. It's usually a small group. It could be up to 50, or 25, even as small as 10. With a group of size, you get to communicate with everybody who's there in a much deeper way than you would do if you're stuck in a vast conference room with 5,000 other delegates.

One thing to be aware of with mastermind groups, and it could be something you need to consider, especially if you've just started and you don't have any immediate funds. To be part of one can be expensive.

What you're paying for is a much more receptive audience, and consequently, your return is much higher, whether be in actual business, fertile network contacts, or learning something that's going to help you grow.

It could well be you may have 20 people in your mastermind group, and you may be the only person who deals with what you do. This can be to your advantage because you can establish whether you can help the other 19 get some extra business. In that room, people expect you to talk about and promote your business, it's what you're there for.

Let's dwell on the cost for a minute. While a mastermind group is incredibly useful, there is no guarantee you'll get business. The costs of participating can be anywhere between $2,000 and $5,000, in some cases, even more. That's a lot of money to find, or even justify when you're starting up in business with little income behind you.

Here's what happened to me, and here's even more evidence of the power of a well-established network of people who you're helping and who are helping you in return.

Through the process of establishing my networks, I made the acquaintance of somebody who was hosting a Mastermind event. We had been communicating for about six months and had no idea of his connection with a Mastermind group. That was a pure coincidence (and, as it turns out, luck on my part).

Our relationship was textbook reciprocation. I asked him a few questions about business, and he answered in detail. In return, he asked me a lot of questions about Facebook advertising, and I answered all of them honestly and openly. I was trying to give my contact as much value as I possibly could.

When the time came for him to host the Mastermind event, he messaged me and asked me if I'd like to take part free of charge. I didn't need to be asked twice. All I had to do was cover my hotel and flights. I was in there!

It's important to understand what I called luck a bit earlier on wasn't luck at all. It was being out there and being open to other people. My invitation to the event typifies why a fertile network is important to you, and why offering value to other people, just helping them, can come back to you in spades. I got invited to an event that, had I decided to pay for myself, would've cost me $3,000.

I was the only Facebook advertiser at the event. In a group of 15 people, I stood out. My contact offered me some great strategies when talking to people at the event, including how to pitch my own services more successfully. This information put me in good stead from then on, and I even managed to do a couple of practice runs while I was at the Mastermind group.

The mastermind led to a significant change to my business. I started charging more for my services without losing any business. At the event, which would have cost me a small fortune (by my standards at the time) to attend, cost me nothing, and I connected with 14 new high-value people. I even made some sales while I was there, which was the icing on the cake.

Normally, I would say making sales *was* the cake, but the quality of the network of contacts I made was superb. I managed to snag some personal development training, and I learned a lot about team building and selling too.

That was five years ago, and I've kept in touch with everybody I met at night. Many of them have introduced me to people who became my customers. In hindsight, had I paid $3,000 to attend, I would not have been unhappy because I got a much bigger return on investment.

My point here is not to say – hey look at me, aren't I great? My point here is about **you**. The point is to dramatically demonstrate the effectiveness of the relationships you develop through networking and to show these relationships could be key in growing your business and making you even more successful.

I know of no business in the world that won't benefit tremendously from a robust and strong network of associates who can mutually help each other. What happened to me could happen to you. In fact, scrap that, if you follow my advice on your network, what happened to me *will* happen to you.

You may be thinking, what if I do get invited to a Mastermind session? What if I'm in a room with people who have businesses worth millions of dollars, and I've barely broken $10,000 in the last six months.

Well, if you're there by invitation of the organizer, he or she knows you as somebody reliable and who has added value to his or her business. They're not going to invite you if that's not the case. If you do get invited, listen to what these people with million-dollar businesses have to say and don't hesitate to pitch in if they mention something you think you can help with.

Terence and the Best Man Speech

Here is another story about the wonderful opportunities a good network can present to you. Terence, the Telephony Guy, is a man who loves writing (he sometimes dreams of living on a remote island and turning out a world-beating novel once every couple of years, just like Ernest Hemingway!).

What happened to him wasn't at a Mastermind event; it was at a seminar with about 500 attendees. He got talking to somebody who he classed as a world-beater in the telephony industry. They talked about their businesses for a while. As the conversation began to dwindle, the man mentioned to Terence he was as nervous as hell because the next day, he was the best man at a wedding and wasn't impressed with his speech.

On a whim, Terence mentioned his writing prowess and offered to look at it for him. The man agreed. And for the next 30 minutes, he and Terence edited and changed some elements of the speech while retaining the core message. At the end of the conversation, his new contact (and almost definite new client thanks to this interchange) said, "Wow, you've made it wittier!"

Two days later, Terence received a bottle of champagne and a thank-you card. Apparently, they loved the speech. This was two years ago, and they keep in regular touch. His contact has offered him some brilliant insight, ideas, and information worth a hundred times the value of his speech rewrite (probably more).

This, of course, demonstrates Mastermind groups are not the only place to meet. There are work conferences, meetings, and seminars relating to either your business or an aspect of your business about which you want to learn more. Check journals and magazines related to your business where these conferences and seminars are advertised in advance. It's well worth keeping an eye on those.

How to Get in Front of Keynote Speakers

One of the best ways to capitalize on a conference is to home in on the keynote speaker, whose subject is pertinent to you. The speaker will more than likely be a leader in his or her field. That's where most people are interested.

What you want to do is talk to him or her and get some insight. But the speakers are usually in high demand. The best way to make yourself known to them is to listen closely to their speech and make notes. If they have books or other literature, go through them. Make sure you're at least familiar with some of it. If you've listened closely to the speaker's talk, then you can greet the speaker in a friendly manner, compliment them on their speech, and then focus on one particular aspect of it. You could say something like, "I've listened to your talk, and it was awesome. I wanted to ask you something about XYZ you were talking about on stage because I found it interesting, particularly when you said ABC."

It's not that just you're letting the speaker know you heard him and appreciated what he said, it also demonstrates a very specific interest in the content, which will make him or her much more responsive to what you have to say. You could then offer to buy a coffee, a drink, or lunch and have a 10-minute conversation about the subject you on which you focused. Remember, **your goal is to approach somebody and discuss something you think will help with your business.**

You'll be surprised at how effective this approach can be used. You're subtly incentivizing the conversation by offering to buy a drink or lunch, and you have mentioned a snippet of time that's only brief. You've shown genuine interest in what the speaker has said, and you've asked him or her for more insight. When your request is genuine, people love being flattered. If I were speaking at one of these groups, and you approached me like this, I would gladly have that drink off you or even a sandwich. (Hint. Hint.)

The conversation you're having is more of a foot in the door at this stage, especially if it's only as brief as 10 minutes or less. If you're in this situation, please avoid using the phrase, "Can I pick your brain?" because immediately makes people think, "If you want to pick my brain, it's going to cost you."

Sometimes at these seminars and conferences, there are breakout sessions where the speaker will host people, and you could attract the attention of the speaker by buying dinner. It's all expensed and tax-deductible. The speaker is the place to be, but there will also be lots of people vying for his or her attention,

However, don't neglect the other people in the room. These breakout sessions might only comprise 20 people, which gives you 20 chances to listen to other people, tell them about yourself, and assess whether you can add value to each other's businesses. If yes, make them part of your network.

The chances are, either in a breakout session or in the wider population of seminar or conference attendees, you're going to have plenty of people in the room with businesses vastly bigger than yours. You just don't know who they are.

Be open to learn and communicate with as many people as you can. Without communication, you're not going to find out there could be somebody sitting next to you who has a business worth millions. Without speaking to him or her, you'll never know.

Remember also, **communication isn't just about talking, it's about constantly listening.** In these conference-type environments, constantly listen, walk around, feel free to interject into people's conversations if you feel it appropriate or if you're not sure what they're talking about. Events like these are huge networking forums. Take advantage of the opportunities as they happen. The conversation could be something totally relevant to you, and you'll find out because you're actively listening.

When you're in these mega-large groups, you almost have to turn yourself into a human antenna picking up signals from all around the room. Listen to everything and jump in when you can. If the person you're speaking with is not interested, politely say goodbye and move on. Jump into a bunch of conversations and go from there. You could make loads of contacts.

Note: I'm saying this as a bonafide introvert. To be a successful business owner, you'll have to find ways to push past your introversion to accomplish your objective. It gets easier with practice, practice, practice.

Admittedly, this is a much easier room with 50 people or less. The book you're reading is the result of a conversation in a hotel restaurant after I spoke at day 2 of a conference.

The key here is to know your own business, know how you want it to grow, and know what resources you have available, whether it be your core product or service of your business or the bank of useful contacts you have forged. Be aware of what you have available to help other people. And be creative. Look at Terence and his speech-writing story.

If you go in with a mindset of wanting to help people, either in small or large ways, the help you give, or even just offer, will start to come back to you tenfold. You're building a reputation as a helpful, trustworthy person, and in a world where there are more cut-throats then there should be, you will stand out.

Let me qualify the last paragraph. I am not saying the business world is full of cut-throats. We do, however, live in a world where some people think the best way to conduct themselves is to be self-centered and have no qualms about exploiting and treading on other people. The business world can be a little bit dog-eat-dog.

However, the reality is most successful businesses foster cooperation, and if you stand out as a decent person who is willing to help other people, it will put you in good stead.

Help isn't just about getting business, at least in the short-term. Help is about reputation, relationships, and reciprocation. It's a great way to be, but let's make no bones about it, helping other people, in the long-term, is about getting business and helping your business grow.

So, you've been to an event, a massive conference, and you've made loads of contacts, what do you do next? First, you have to think deeply about the nature of the conversation you've had with each of the delegates. Could any of these conversations lead to a sale soon? Make these new prospects your number one priority to contact.

With the rest, think about what they do and what you do. Think about what you can offer each other. But don't confine yourself to pure sales. Think about what you could learn from this contact, what contacts they might have, and vice-versa, what they could learn from you and somebody in your contacts might help them.

For example, if you're in the recruitment business, they might know somebody who oversees recruitment for a large firm you may be able to help. For Terence, it might be somebody who has knowledge of an aspect of software development for his new system. Each situation is going to be different.

At the event itself, if you tell people about the services you offer, even if they're not necessarily potential buyers, they may know somebody who may be a potential buyer. Someone might say, "I know somebody who could use your help," and they will introduce you. Because they present you as a person who can help, it becomes a much easier conversation.

Also, when you're talking to people, take as many notes as you can. It can be a bit rude if you're doing in conversation, but as soon as the conversation finishes, write your notes. The more information you collect and retain, the easier it will be to work out how you can help each other.

THE FOLLOW-UP

A phrase I often hear is, "The money is in the follow-up," and in my experience, this is 100% true. What's the point of having these conversations that could lead to something if you then don't follow it through? You're relying on people following through with you, and most times, people will forget. You need to be the leader in this process.

Let's say you meet somebody. The notes you take should include what they do, what they specialize in, how you think they can help you, and how you can help them. You don't need large volumes of information but important bullet points and keywords to help jog your memory. These notes will be invaluable.

At a bigger venue spanning a few days, you could have up to 100 of these types of conversations. That's why it's important to make notes on each one. Otherwise, all the conversations will meld together.

When it comes to conversation, it's important to strike while the iron is hot or should I say strike while the connection is hot. You need to send follow-up messages no more than a few days later. Let's say you're at an event for four days, from Thursday to Sunday, and back at your desk on Monday, ready and raring to contact these people.

Let's stick to the realistic idea that you have 100 people to follow up with. Sitting at your desk on Monday morning, with all the other things going on in your business, that's a lot of work. But you must do it while your conversation is still fresh in their minds, and you have to get those messages sent by Monday or Tuesday at the latest if you met them on the previous Thursday.

If you leave it for more than a week, then chances are you have missed some opportunities. Bear in mind your contacts will also have had lots of conversations at the conference too, and the longer you leave it, the less of a memory your contact will have of you.

Any message I send is accompanied by a picture embedded in my email, text, or however, I send it. This helps jog the memory. This is what my email/text contains, other than the message itself: My name, telephone number, email address, a link to my website, a small image of me, and finally a little message at the bottom which says "Facebook Ads Master."

All these things serve two purposes for the recipient: First, they act as a memory jogger, and second, they make it very easy for the recipient to get back to me.

Some people like emails, while some prefer texts. If you've established information in your brief meeting, respond in whatever way your new contact prefers. Remember, **everything is about making the recipient of your messages want to respond to you.** If you use a method of communication they prefer, the chances of happening increase.

If you're not sure, just email, but either way, just get it done as quickly as you can. Also, assume you're going to get some responses straight away and plan to deal with those responses as quickly as you can. You need to jump on those messages too.

Let's say you send 100 messages in the first couple of days, and 40 people respond. Every response opens the door to reinitiating those conversations, from which could spring more opportunities and potential new business. That's why you must plan your workload to cope with demand immediately.

The Follow-Up Message Content

The purpose of the content is usually an attempt to continue the conversation started at the conference. Your message should be short, sweet, and attention-grabbing. You could send something like this (though I heartily recommend crafting your own to suit your situation):

"I enjoyed our conversation at the conference/seminar (or wherever you met) around ABC, and I'd love to expand a little more on and talk about XYZ."

The first part, ABC, is the subject discussed by the contact, and the second part, XYZ, is what you want to talk about. This could be anything pertinent to your business.

Let me give you an example of a message sent to somebody in real estate. As I've said, it's one of my long-term aspirations.

"Hey. Brian, thank you so much for everything at the event. I'd love to continue our conversation concerning real estate investing because it's something I've wanted to do for years, and I feel like you're the go-to person for this. By the same token, I'd love to have a conversation around Facebook advertising because I feel this could help grow your business. I'll even throw in a couple of tactics work for clients in a similar position to you the next time we talk. Do you have a booking link to book a call, or would you prefer I send you mine? Let me know."

Simple, straightforward, and attention-grabbing.

Always try to use a scheduler too, because you have lots of these calls to make. If they send you their scheduler, it's like sending you to their personal assistant and the equivalent of "Yes, we can talk." People don't send you to their scheduler if they don't want to talk to you.

Staying with the Emails

First, let's just say you don't manage to make those initial contacts, those emails, or texts within the first two to three days. There are a couple of reasons for this. One is because you've just got so many of them to do (a nice problem to have). Or, it could be because when you get back from the

155

conference, you're assaulted by a bunch of emergencies. Your baby is not very well, your mother is ill, or your car breaks down permanently, and you have to spend a couple of days handling your personal fires. Anything from the grand spectacle of life.

You may be thinking since you haven't contacted these people in a timely enough fashion, it's probably not worth it now. You couldn't be more wrong.

While it's true, the longer you leave it, the less likely people are to respond, if through unforeseen circumstances you have to wait for a week or two or even a month, you're still likely to get some level of response. And that's what you're after. The quicker you do it, the better. Don't give up because you weren't able to initiate the messages within a couple of days.

Save Yourself Some Time

To save you time in the follow-up, do the following:

1. Standardize and templatize your response, gives you less to think about.

2. If you're at a conference for three to four days, (especially if you're staying in a hotel and have some downtime), if you get thirty contacts on one day, spend evening drafting out as many as you can.

3. Send as many responses as you can each evening.

4. That means on Monday, instead of having to do all the work for 100 contacts, you've written 50 drafts, and for all of those quickly double-check the email and send it

off. A task might have taken you all Monday has only taken you a couple of hours.

5. You then should have no problem in dealing with the remaining 50 by the end of Tuesday.

The figures are hypothetical, the point is to make the job as easy as possible, and GET IT DONE.

How many times should you attempt to make contact?

This is not scientific, but I would say four times, sometimes five.

- **First email/text.** sent on Monday. If there's no response:

- **Second email.** Resubmit on Wednesday of that week, but forward it and say something like, "Hey, I just wanted to make sure you received this email sent on Monday, and it didn't go into your spam file. I've pasted the message below."

- **Third email.** Another 48 hours have passed. Send a message on Friday. This time, change the subject of your email, preferably to something that will catch the attention of the sender. Even something silly like "I heard this about you..." and then when they open the email it's a smiley face and a message saying "I heard you're grrrreat! I'd like to have a conversation with you. If not, totally fine, just let me know by responding, yes or no. But if you have 10 minutes to speak on what we talked about at the event, I'd love to have something on the calendar. Let me know the next best steps." While it sounds silly, it does catch the attention, and it makes people read the content of the entire message, which is what you want them to do.

- **Fourth and final email.** This should be on the following Monday, a whole week after your first message. Change the subject line again. Make it something like, "I was thinking about you when I had this idea" or "I had this thought about you..." Hopefully, the curiosity-driven headline will make them open it again, and you might write something like "I would feel this is the last time I'm going to email you, I just want to know whether there is an opportunity for me to speak to you for just five minutes or even just a couple of minutes to continue our conversation from the event on XYZ. Let me know either way."

In the last message, there's no more joking around. It's just, "Would you like to talk – yes or no?" written in a polite way still designed to get their attention.

Should you decide to email anymore, keep changing the subject line. For me, four is the maximum in one week. If I've sent four messages and received no response, that's ok; it's time to move on because there are plenty of other people to contact.

The only other thing I might do, and this would be my fifth attempt, if you emailed them, is to add them on Facebook or LinkedIn (or text them) and send the first message again. If they don't respond, then it is time to move on permanently.

How to deal with the people who respond to you

First, congratulations. Second, I have used the following figures. From 100 messages, I received 40 responses. It's taken time to grow my numbers. Don't be disappointed if you receive lower response rates, even significantly less. I have come up with the figure 40 from 100 through a whole pile of trial and error over several years. Each business is different, and as you practice this and get better, you will establish your own response rate and improve on it!

Either way, you should apply the same level of speediness to these responses as you did to the original messages. Schedule the conversation as soon as you can. Usually, these conversations are about 15 minutes long, but if after 15 minutes you realize you have a lot more to talk about (and this should be a mutual realization), then you schedule another call, this time for 30 minutes or as long as you feel is appropriate.

Another thing, if you schedule a call, don't miss it under any circumstances. But, conversely, if your contact is late, forgets, or wants to reschedule, be gracious about it.

Never forget the purpose of the calls – to establish how you can help your new contact and how they can help you.

I will conclude this chapter by stating our three Ps, patience, persistence, and practice, all apply to the concept of forging relationships. And if you follow what I'm doing here, and if you take it as seriously as I do, I can assure you that you will have loads more contacts, your business will improve, your knowledge will improve, and you will grow your business.

CHAPTER 5

Step 5 – Financial Literacy

PART 1: YOUR GROWTH

Welcome to Step 5, covering all financial aspects. I'm not just talking about finances for the business. I'm talking about finances for your entire life. As an entrepreneur running your own business, your personal and business finances are inextricably linked.

There are three sections to this chapter because, though every step we have talked about so far is critical to the success of your business, I firmly believe finances are the foundation. Ironically, the main point of going into business is to make yourself lots of money, yet the actual management of money and finances generally is the least sexy part of the whole endeavor.

Accountants get a bad rap, but without one, or without employing the same skills to your business an accountant would, your business will soon flounder. Whether you consider yourself good with money or not, numbers don't lie.

In these three sections, we're going to be looking at three discrete aspects of your finances.

1. **Personal growth.** This deals with the notion of making enough money for you to survive, plus having a couple of emergency funds accrued.

2. **Investing for growth.** In this section, we'll be looking beyond the time when you're earning enough money to survive and save emergency funds to the time when you're making enough money to invest back into your business, and therefore, you're looking at putting your business into overdrive.

3. **Maintenance.** In the final section on finances, we'll be looking at ways to maintain your current status and invest in your long-term future.

PERSONAL GROWTH

Personal growth is about investing in yourself. Of course, everything could be defined as investing in yourself, but in this section, we'll be taking a close look at your personal finances and the best way to manage them. Looking at several distinct areas, it is my firm belief before you make your business grow as much as you can, or invest in it fully, you need to take care of your own personal finances and make sure you're on a firm footing.

There are four aspects to this. First, the sudden crisis fund. Second, how to work out your monthly survival fund. Third, the survival fund itself, how much it should be, and where you should keep it. Fourth, the emergency fund.

One final thing before we get on to them. The point of creating these funds is so that you can safely, without stress, work hard on your business. Without having these funds in place, your lack of financial literacy could negatively affect your business. You're about to learn how to avoid that trap.

The Sudden Crisis Fund

This is a small but critical part of your personal savings. In "The Plight of the Millennial" in the introduction of this book, I mentioned that 50% of Millennials, should they have an urgent need for over $500, wouldn't be able to cover it. I'm talking about things like a car breakdown, the washing machine malfunctioning, or needing an emergency plumber. Substitute any number of issues that have happened in the last few years.

The sudden crisis fund is to have between $500 to $1,000 in it. Accrue this fund first so that you can work on the other funds. Have it in an account separate from your checking account, but one you can get access to immediately. Immediacy is a trademark of a sudden crisis. We don't need to dwell on this too long, and the good news is, once you start accruing money into your survival fund, you could consider rolling your sudden crisis fund into the next fund.

The Survival Fund

The survival fund and the emergency fund are not to be confused. The survival fund is the cash you need every month multiplied by six. This fund is so that you can continue living your current lifestyle for six months, even if your business is going through a dry patch.

The emergency fund, although it sounds similar, is not the same. This is essentially another six-month pot of savings. On top of the six months of accrued expenses, add any excess charges for your various insurances. Actually, it's kind of like your own insurance. We'll come back to this fund soon. For now, let's concentrate on the survival fund first.

How to Work Out Your Survival Fund

It's important to do this sequentially. Once you've taken care of your emergency crisis fund, the survival fund comes next. How do you know what your survival fund is? You would be amazed at how few people know what it is, let alone how to work it out.

Keep it simple. What you're trying out is how much money you will need to survive for six months without earning any additional money.

1. Take all your bills over the year. Box off the monthly bills first because that's how most bills are paid nowadays. Make sure you don't miss anything. The list includes water, electricity, phone bills, Wi-Fi access,

rent, mortgage, ground rent, credit cards, student loans, TV subscriptions (like Netflix), Amazon Prime, and house insurance. The list goes on and on. Write them down and add them up. Better still, enter them into MS Excel, Google Sheets, or some electronic spreadsheet and let the software do all the heavy calculations for you.

2. Enter all the bills you pay yearly, or quarterly, or every six months. Things like a gym membership, car maintenance, insurance, and have a monthly figure for these as well. You want to boil it down to a monthly figure. If you pay a bill yearly, you want to divide it into 12, if you pay a bill quarterly, into thirds.

3. This one might be a bit harder and may involve a degree of estimating. The definition of estimating is "taking an educated guess." We're talking about food, socializing, and anything that has an ad-hoc feel to it. Do your best to come up with a figure, and if you're not sure, add 10% to the figure you come up with to be on the safe side. Again, break this down to a monthly figure. How much do you spend on food? Then add your groceries. If you or your kids like a weekly or daily McDonald's trip, you might have to do a little bit of estimation here, but you need to put a reasonable figure in and divide the annual figure by 12.

4. Add your monthly bills total to the monthly figure you have calculated for your other bills, to the monthly figure you have calculated for your food, socializing, and miscellaneous. This total figure is the money you need to survive for one month.

5. Multiply the figure by six. That, ladies and gentlemen, is your survival fund. If your business has a slow couple of months, you have a savings to tap into until business picks up. And when it does, replenish your survival fund.

Forgive this aside, I am amazed at how many people are not sure of the dates their payments are due to come out and sometimes even the amounts. For those people with a full-time job and a regular healthy income, that's a reasonable amount over their monthly bills, that's understandable, but still not ideal.

For those in business, you must know where every scrap of your money is being spent and precisely when it leaves your account. Undertaking this exercise to establish your survival fund and reviewing when your bills come out has a healthy collateral effect. It prompts you to ask yourself whether you're spending money wisely. If you reduce your monthly spending, you reduce your survival fund. It's not the first aim of this process, but something to consider when you know all of your numbers.

Do you need a survival fund and a crisis fund? Not necessarily, at least when you've nearly accrued all of your survival funds. Personally, I think having little crisis amount is sensible all the way through accruing your survival and emergency funds. But the survival fund is the first major amount to save.

Most people will want to keep their survival fund in an account that's completely discrete from their checking account. My advice would be to keep it separated, at least until you've accrued 90% of your survival fund.

If you're not used to saving, make it a habit. I guarantee you, if you don't and your earnings dwindle, you could find your business in financial trouble. Keep the fund filled.

Keeping Track. I do everything by spreadsheet. Everything. I keep track of all my contacts by spreadsheet, as well as my finances. I personally favor Microsoft Excel but know many entrepreneurs who swear by Google Sheets.

Either way, you must make a habit of keeping meticulous track of your finances. Let the spreadsheet do all the work. Learning the formulas you need is pretty straightforward. There are plenty of references for this available. YouTube has some great videos on managing spreadsheets, and it's all free.

Set aside a small amount of time every day for reviewing and managing your finances, especially if you haven't done regularly in the past. Once you get used to it, it will only take about 20 minutes a day. If you're scrutinizing your daily finances, you will soon start to learn when to expect your bills, and exactly how much is coming out. This is important if your income from your business is coming through intermittently, and you haven't quite got your survival fund in place yet.

How to Build Up Your Fund. Keep it simple. Put all of the profit from your business into it. Thus, the more you put in, the quicker your fund will build up. But don't worry, if you're at the stage where you're making a small amount of profit, just put what you can in. Even then, you'll be surprised at how much you have at the end of the year. You just have to devote your full profit to it.

You should have a checking account, a savings account for your taxes, and then an account for your survival fund. It's also best to have an account for your survival fund that doesn't have immediate access but a cooling off period of, say, 24 hours. Once you get to the correct amount, it's time to move on to the emergency fund.

The Emergency Fund

This fund is ostensibly similar to the survival fund but has a completely different function. What happens if you fall over and break your leg, or some other mishap befalls you? What happens if you contract glandular fever, and you're laid low for three months?

Anything that keeps you out of action for anything more than a month is a problem, because, currently, you're a one-man-band.

This is the purpose of your emergency fund – to cover such eventualities. It also has six months of savings, just like the survival fund. Plus, you put an extra bit in for any deductibles or excesses from your insurances. Most insurance plans have deductibles. The plan may cover all but 10% of your bills. That 10% in this example is your deductible, and if you're out of action for two to three months, it can be quite a stack of money. To be safe, you must add a little something on top of your emergency fund. Aim for another quarter.

A couple of people have said to me, "Isn't this just a duplication of the survival fund? Why can't you use one fund for both?" The answer to the first question is an emphatic no, it's different from the survival fund, and the answer to the second question is clear-cut, too.

Let's just say, for health reasons, you've had to take somewhere between three and six months off. Lucky you, you heeded my advice and put away six months of money and a quarter more to cover any health costs. On your return to work, as a small business operator, you will have inevitably lost some business. Your customers may have gone elsewhere in your absence. To get back to your original position, you'll hustle harder for a few months. Luckily, you also took my advice on having a separate survival fund to cover your business deficits.

Do you see the importance of separate accounts? A single six-month fund won't cover a realistic scenario.

To summarize our discussion so far, I'm going to pluck some figures out of the air for demonstration purposes only.

Let's say your monthly expenditures are $3,000. Your survival fund is going to be $18,000. Your emergency fund is going to be $22,500 on top of that. That's another $18,000 plus $4,500 for medical expenses, which is an extra 25%.

All in all, you need to save $40,500, plus $1,000 for your sudden crisis fund, should you choose to carry it on, making a total of $41,500.

If your monthly figure is $2,500, your total savings for both funds plus the crisis fund would be $34,750.

If your monthly figure were $2,000, the total figure would be $28,000

If your monthly figure were $1,500, your total figure would be $21,250. You can see saving on your monthly bills could translate to a significantly smaller amount. Even saving $100 would reduce the figure by over $1,300.

It's at this stage you can potentially look over your monthly spending for places to save money. For instance, things like Netflix or your gym membership. Ask yourself if you can do away with these, thus reducing your survival and emergency fund. But that's for you to decide. A big principle here is to have this money set aside in separate accounts.

To recap, the accounts you will need:

- Checking account for your bills.
- Savings account for your taxes.
- Savings account for your crisis fund with immediate access.
- Savings account for your survival fund with 24-hour access.
- Savings account for your emergency fund with 24-hour access.

Once you fill these funds, you can breathe a sigh of relief and move on to Phase 2 of your financial literacy. However, you'll also need a survival fund and a separate emergency fund for your business. It probably won't be anywhere near as much but could include things like separate Wi-Fi, web domain provider, funds, etc. At this point, it would be a good idea to have the survival and emergency funds in separate savings accounts that give you immediate access.

FINANCIAL LITERACY –
PART 2: INVESTING FOR GROWTH

The Freedom Fund

You have your survival and emergency fund in place. Should the bottom fall out of your business, you've got a six-month cushion to recover. Should you break your arm in a skiing accident, or your ankle in the park, you've got a fund to cover too. It's a good place to be, and a good feeling, because now you can start investing the extra income you earn for growth.

You have some freedom. That's why I call this money your freedom fund. It's what you have leftover once your monthly bills are paid. Another, more familiar name for it is disposable income. But I hate that name. The word "disposable" trivializes it.

It's time to start investigating the best way to spend this money to grow your business and make more money.

Here are some generic suggestions that cover some of the items Terence and I have used our freedom funds for:

- Extra staff
- New equipment and new PCs
- More efficient software
- Training courses
- Mastermind session

It all depends on your own business, but when considering any of the above or any number of the hundreds of things you could spend your extra money on, you have to consider this. Whether it's contributing to growing your business and even whether it's directly paying for itself, in many ways, it should just be paying for itself.

Let me give you two examples.

Terence had decided it might be a good idea for him to procure some more PA equipment. He had been turning down requests for PA rentals for a couple of months and worked out one day that, had he had the proper equipment, he could've rented nine sets in one night. Averaging it out, he reckoned over four days he could have hired out three PA systems, plus booked a DJ, or even acted as DJ himself.

An entire PA system, including lights, isn't cheap, and he didn't have the funding for it, but he went for it anyway. He didn't compromise on quality. He decided to shop around for deals.

Instead of spending $4,000 on specific equipment, he managed to source it for $2,500. Top marks to Terence. He purchased one set at a time and let it pay for itself through extra bookings before buying another set.

Within four weeks, he'd recouped half of the money he spent. The problem was that he was still turning business down. So, he took some of the extra income he was making from the other two strands of his business, telephony and computer repair, and invested in another PA set. Once the first set was paid for completely, he invested in the third set because he was getting an average of three bookings on a Friday and Saturday night, and two on a Sunday. What a great way to grow his business and the perfect use of his freedom fund.

A second example. Maybe you've set up a print shop, and you've priced up a new printer, which will give you greater capacity and enable you to execute higher volume, higher spec work. You've taken the extra cost of the machine, calculated the value of the extra work you would need, and factored in some marketing costs to get this extra work. You've worked out to break even it would take 17 months. And, you ask yourself, is it worth it? If you think it is, then you make the investment, if you don't think it is because you can think of better, quicker ways to grow the business, then don't.

Although it's a little harder, you can estimate the Return on Investment (ROI) on a training course or even a Mastermind session. Again, if you think the investment is going to increase your business and you think it's worth it, go for it. If not, don't. But you need to continue to look at ways to use your freedom fund to expand your business.

I would always advise, before spending any of your funds, do what Terence did, and try to source things more cheaply (without compromising on quality). When it comes to training, in particular, be stringent and look for other avenues first. Have you tried looking online? Podcasts and YouTube training videos are all over the internet nowadays, or even an e-book, or if you want to go old-school, a good old-fashioned book with actual pages!

That's how I learned SEO. I didn't pay a penny for training, but I did spend a lot of hours learning. If you can spare the time, and find the courses, your ROI questions should revolve around whether it's worth your time to learn this new skill yourself, or is it better to invest in a course, thus fast-tracking your learning.

If you can save money, then do it. If you think the benefits of the course outweigh the costs, and the time it might take to source good material and train yourself, then buy the course. Business is fun, and decisions like this are the best part of the process because you're in the exciting part of your business where you're scaling up. But...

WHAT ABOUT DEBT?

In my mind, I'm thinking about all of the student loan debt Millennials are saddled with. Debt will follow you until it's paid, even if you go bankrupt.

You may be thinking if you're earning all this money in your freedom fund, wouldn't it be sensible to pay off debt? Yes, partially, but you need to grow and scale your business. If you do this successfully, you'll be able to pay off any outstanding debts with ease in the coming years. Still, something is satisfying about paying off long-term debt, and you do save on interest.

It's your decision. Perhaps you want to think about allocating a portion of your freedom fund to debt, say 20%, and the rest to grow your business. Or 30%, or whatever you're more comfortable with. Just understand the more you allocate to debt relief, the less you have to grow your business, and therefore, the slower your growth may be, until, of course, your debt is paid off.

What else could you spend your freedom fund on? Sometimes it's difficult to be completely accurate when predicting ROI. Perhaps you want to try recruiting new staff because you're convinced it will bring in extra revenue will pay for the cost of the staff, and then some.

It's going to cost you $1,000 per month (another figure plucked out of the air to illustrate my point). You're going to try it for six months and then review. You must commit. Once you do, $6,000 is spent, and you should no longer worry about it. If you have a quiet first month, don't fret or stew about it. The decision you have already made (to go for it) should free you from emotional setbacks. At the end of the trial period, assess thoroughly. You either decide it was a commercial flop and let them go, or that it was a commercial success and make the new staff a permanent part of your monthly expenditures.

Other things to invest in to help grow your business are things I've already mentioned. E-commerce, affiliate marketing, your own books or downloadable training packages, podcasts, blogs, etc., all of which are aimed at increasing your brand awareness, your knowledge, the size of your business, your revenue, and your profit.

Some of the above are time-consuming but low in cost. Just keep doing it, keep slogging away, and working out the best ways to grow.

FINANCIAL LITERACY –
PART 3: MAINTENANCE

Maintenance is about your long-term wealth. This is the holy grail, where you have scaled your business up to the point where you have even more disposable income. Instead of having a six-month emergency and/or survival fund, you've accrued up to three years, maybe more.

The decisions you need to make now revolve around whether you want all money you're making to be devoted to making more money, or whether you want to save it, whether you want to build generational wealth for your family to inherit, or whether you want to do all three.

If you want your money to make more money you could:

- **Start new businesses or invest in other peoples' businesses.** It's time-consuming and potentially risky because you may have to learn new skills, which can be time-consuming or pay somebody with those skills, which can be expensive, and in the meantime, it could take you away from your own business, which still has a lot of growth potential.

- **You could invest in stocks.** There are several ways of doing this. One is the old-fashioned way of buying stocks in companies you think will grow.

- **Index funds.** This is another more hassle-free way of investing. You can either invest in the market as a whole or invest in a cluster of stocks. With both of these scenarios, you usually (but not always) receive a quarterly dividend.

- **A combination of stocks and index funds.**

- **Automated investment services. Also known as robo-advisors.** This is said to be the next big thing. These are companies crowd-fund the efforts of different experts. You don't even have to know where the investments are going, you just put in as much as you see fit, and the robo-advisers do the rest of the work. At the end of each year, you get a return on your investments. Compared to banks (with a return of 1%), many companies, such as Wealthfront, have been bringing an annual return of 2.5%. But there are also robo-advisors for real estate, for art, for almost everything.

- **Real estate.** It can take a lot of money to invest, but the returns are generally higher than most other investment techniques.

A general run-down of returns on investment.

Bear in mind these are historical figures. There's no guarantee you'll get the same returns in the future.

- Robo-advisors (stock only) – 2.5%

- Savings account – 1%

- Real estate – 5 to 10%

- Stocks generally – 3-7% over the last decade.

Other factors include how much you have to invest (although with most robo-advisors you can invest as little as

$1,000 if you want) and the level of risk. While a savings account is by far the lowest return, it is the safest.

I am no expert in this matter. I stress all of the above figures are subject to change, and I would seriously advise you to get some impartial financial advice before embarking on any of the above ventures.

Just consider this. Say you have $100,000 to invest. That investment spread over 30 years with a growth of 4% will end up being over $300,000.

You should only do this type of investing once you've followed the sequence. Let's say you have $100k to invest, and let's say you lose it all (an unlikely scenario). If you've got all your other things buckled down, your survival and emergency funds, but maybe stretching for a year, and you've still got money in your freedom fund to invest in your business, you will have lost an awful lot but not everything. You can still live comfortably, and you can still continue to make more money from your business or businesses.

That's the thing about investments. You should only invest if you're comfortable with losing. It's a game of mathematics and chance. If the idea of losing money stresses you out, maybe you want to consider a safer avenue for your wealth.

You could, for instance, decide you don't want six months as a survival and emergency fund, you want three years, or even five. Wow. If you did, you would truly feel comfortable. One concept I've learned from networking with wealthy individuals is that they value time over money. They measure their wealth by the amount of time they can buy. Three to five years of expenses in an account is a decent amount of wealth.

I also mentioned building investments for your family's future. You could set up an IRA (Individual Retirement Account) for yourself. You could set up 529 college plans for your children, and make sure there's enough in there to make a difference to them. Being saddled with student loan debt is not a good way to be. Wouldn't it be great to help your children avoid the scenario? Or you could set up a Roth IRA plan for them, or a fund they can only access when they're 18, 21, or 25, or whatever age you deem suitable.

Keep the same daily control and knowledge over your finances as you did when you were building up your survival fund. That way, should you choose to splash out on luxury items, like a Lamborghini, or a villa in Cancun, you'll know you can afford them. Each level of wealth buys you more freedom.

Imagine replacing yourself. The eventual freedom is, of course, to stop working. You could hand over the reins of your business to somebody else. This could happen when your investments are giving you the income you need. You've achieved this success through your businesses. You also have a fantastic asset to sell (your business) and accrue even more wealth.

BONUS CHAPTER

How to Be an Entrepreneur and Stay Healthy

Being an entrepreneur has lots of perks, but there are some pitfalls to avoid. One of them is the juggle between working hard and staying healthy. When piling on the hours, it's all too easy to fall into undesirable habits that could adversely affect your health in the short-, medium-, and long-term. For example, these are some behaviors to avoid.

- Quickly grabbing a snack or junk food instead of eating healthily.

- Working late and getting up early to work some more. Who needs to sleep? You do!

- Sitting at a desk for long stretches and not getting enough, or any, exercise.

Let me be as blunt as I can be. Adapting any of the behaviors above is bad for you and will cause health issues in the long run. Adapting two or all three is a sure-fire ticket to an early grave.

The secret to avoiding health issues is this: Eat well, exercise well, and sleep well. Achieving all three is not as difficult as it sounds, it's just good habits. Achieving all three will reduce the chances of you ever needing to use your emergency fund. Achieving all three will make you more productive and be good for your business.

Let's take each facet one-by-one.

Eating Well

Eating well does not involve you trashing all the foods you like, nor does it involve you going on difficult, semi-starvation diets.

It's about making sure you avoid as much sugar and refined flour as you can. Yes, if you binge on sugary snacks and potato snacks, I advise you to drastically reduce or even eliminate these from your diet. Sugar is a killer.

Too much of it induces obesity, heart disease, high blood pressure, strokes, and dementia. The government recommends no more than 9 teaspoons, or 37.5 grams for men, and 6 teaspoons, or 25 grams for women. That is not a lot.

Let's put it into perspective. There are 27 grams of sugar in a glazed donut. That's right. Just one glazed donut.

Add to that the amount of hidden sugar in most products, even food like canned soup. Avoiding sugar as much as possible will be the single most important nutritional habit you can take on. Watch out for fruits as well. Although it contains natural sugar, the liver is not very good at distinguishing between natural and refined sugar. Too much of it can be just as bad for you.

Avoid eating anything that raises your blood sugar levels too high. Blood sugar, also known as glucose, is used as an energy source, but if your blood sugar levels go too high for too long, it can play havoc with the body's internal organs. Worse, it can bring on a condition called insulin resistance. Talk about a vicious feedback loop. Insulin resistance is caused by constantly too-high blood sugar levels but also makes those blood sugar levels go even higher. If it happens, you're in danger of becoming diabetic (a nasty condition which can result in blindness, limb amputations, and a shorter lifespan) strokes, heart disease, and dementia.

Eat plenty of root vegetables. They are crammed full of vitamins and nutrients that make you feel better and are full of fiber, which means they have little impact on blood sugar levels.

Exercise Well

You don't have to exercise like an Olympic athlete to be healthy. All you need to do is devote half-an-hour a day to some cardiovascular exercise and do a couple of strengthening (weight) exercises per week. I won't dwell on the negatives if you don't (it's the same list of life-threatening ailments I mentioned if you don't eat well), but if you exercise regularly, you will live longer, feel better, be more alert, and get more done.

Government guidelines suggest you should do 150 minutes or more of moderate activity every week. That boils down to half an hour a day. The good news is you can do this in chunks. If you went for a walk for 10 minutes every two hours in six hours, that would be it. The kind of exercise we're talking about here includes brisk walking, moderate cycling, moderate cross-trainer activity, or even half-an-hour of gardening, as long as it raises your heart rate to the point where you can feel it.

Strength exercises should be done twice a week and should include exercising all the major muscles.

Sleep Well

This is sometimes the hardest one to achieve. Some people, even if they have good habits, still find it difficult to switch off at night. The list of things below will help you get a good night's sleep. They require discipline but are worth the effort.

- Go to bed and wake up at the same time every day.
- Reduce caffeine intake ten hours before you go to bed.
- Increase exposure to daylight during waking hours.
- Cut down on long naps during the day.
- Cut down on alcohol. Betters still, avoid it.
- Make sure your bedroom is dark and devoid of any red or blue lights from electronics.

- Keep the room as cool as you can stand. The body's temperature needs to drop slightly before deep sleep induces.

- Avoid late-night eating. Stop at least two hours before bed.

- Relax before going to bed. Go through an evening routine.

- Create a comfortable environment. Make sure your bed, blankets, and pillows are comfortable.

- Exercise regularly (but not a couple of hours before you go to bed.)

The three cornerstones of a healthy life – sleeping, eating, and exercise – are interlinked. Sleeping well will make you feel more inclined to exercise and is shown to reduce obesity. Exercising and eating healthy will make you sleep better.

None of this means you have to work fewer hours if you're inclined to work long hours. It does mean you shouldn't pull all-nighters, and it means you should stop working a couple of hours before you go to bed, but that's about it. You can be a successful entrepreneur *and* live a long, healthy life!

Another thing that will contribute to your emotional well-being is how well prepared you are with your new business. I have one final checklist for you, which acts as a summary for much of what we've discussed in this book and an honorable mention for other aspects of running a business that will help you.

- Make sure you eventually choose a business that fits you.

- Make sure there is a market out there for you to sell to.

- Do your homework on your competitors. You may think your niche or product is totally unique. To ensure the success of your business, you need to become as knowledgeable as possible about what your competitors offer, how they sell their products or services, how your offering compares, and what makes your offering unique. Also, your competitors' businesses are likely to evolve and change as much as yours does, so assessing your competition should be an ongoing task.

- Make sure you give equal billing to how your business runs (the operational side) and the selling side. Many businesses have stumbled because they have sold well but not been able to deliver what they sell, thanks to a poorly organized infrastructure.

- Plan and plan for success. You don't need to do a 5- or 10-year plan as recommended by most MBAs, but a tangible, specific, and achievable set of targets, ones can be translated into incremental actions. And make sure your plan projects success.

- Set a start date for your new business and stick to it without fail. Have you ever heard of analysis paralysis? Prospective new business owners can fall into this trap as they investigate every nook and cranny of starting their new business. This bout of major procrastination is understandable, starting a new business is a big thing, and can cause anxiety. The truth is every new business learns as it goes along. There's nothing wrong with due process but not at the expense of unnecessary delays. Pick a date and stick to it. You won't regret it.

- Start small; plan big.

- Learn from your mistakes. Never beat yourself up.

- Learn as much as you can from other people. I've covered this at length.

- Take care of the finances. See previous chapters.

- Learn and exploit digital marketing. Today, the lion's share of my business is all about digital marketing, but no matter what you do, whether you're a dog groomer or a drop shipper, a plumber, or a book writer, it would be a mistake to ignore digital marketing. That's where most people look for any services or products they require.

- Stay open to learning. Never stop trying new things.

- Network, network, network.

- Get comfortable with the notion of having people work for you. This might be one of the hardest things to get used to. You may achieve a modicum of success if you do everything yourself as a one-man band, but if you want to build your business and expand, you will need a team around you.

  - Start on a small scale before going all out.

•

CONCLUSION

We've covered all five steps. Our journey is almost over. Before leaving my closing remarks, here's a reminder of the steps we've covered:

- **Step 1.** Getting started, identifying the low-hanging fruit, and choosing the right business.

- **Step 2.** The three Ps of longevity – Practice, Patience, and Persistence.

- **Step 3.** Deciding on your business model.

- **Step 4.** Forging productive relationships.

- **Step 5.** Financial literacy.

If you're still eager to start your own business (and I hope you are), it's now up to you. Everything starts with a decision. That's it. If you decide to start a new business, you will do everything in your power to make it happen, and one decision will be the start of and driver to hundreds, even thousands, of other decisions down the line.

I presume you have read this book and have been thinking about starting a business because you recognize the need to change something in your life. But if you don't decide to do something, then nothing will change for you.

The decision to start a new business is also a decision to believe in yourself, to act, to take risks, and to develop a plan. The decision to spend a quarter of your time, half, or devote your entire energy to your new venture will have consequences for the speed of your business's success. But it comes down to this.

It starts with a decision. The decision to do it, to go for it, and from everything brilliance grows. I hope you go for it, and I wish you all the luck in the world.

REFERENCES

Angone, P. (ND). 5 Shocking Statistics About Real "Millennial Problems" (and how we overcome). Retrieved from https://allgroanup.com

Attard, J. (2019, August 15). 16 Tips for Starting and Succeeding in Your Own Business. Retrieved from https://businessknowhow.com

Bestwork, I. (2018, August). The Ten Most Serious Problems Facing Millennials. Retrieved from www.bestworkinc.com

Department of Health. (2018, June 11). Benefits of Exercise. Retrieved from www.nhs.co.uk

Eliason, N. (2017, March 29). What Life Do You Want? Retrieved from www.nateliason.com

Global internet usage. (2019, May 24). Retrieved from https://en.wikipedia.org/wiki/Global_Internet_usage

Gregory, A. (2019, April 12). 12 Tips for Making Your Business Blog a Success. Retrieved from https://www.the balancesmb.com

Hoffower, H. (2019, May 21). 6 financial problems plaguing Millennials through no fault of their own. Retrieved from www.businessinsider.com

Kraly, A. (2019, January 2). The truth about Amazon drop shipping: Should you be selling on Amazon?. Retrieved from www.dropshiplifestyle.com

Mawer, R. (2019, November 2). 17 Proven Tips to Sleep Better

At night. Retrieved from https://healthline.com

Singal, A. (2018, January 11). How to Start Affiliate Marketing (+Best Affiliate Programs for 2019). Retrieved from www.lurn.com

Theobald, L. (2018, January 30). How aspirational content will help you sell more. Retrieved from https://blog.usefetch.io

Todrin, D. (2012, April 20). 7 Ways to Ensure Your Business Succeeds. Retrieved from https://entrepreneur.com/

ABOUT THE AUTHOR

David Schloss was born and raised in Miami, FL and began his entrepreneurial journey back in 2007 from his college apartment.

Over the years, he has helped hundreds of businesses improve their website visibility, customer acquisition, and revenue using social advertising.

His agency, Convert ROI (www.convertroi.com), enables businesses to succeed by taking complicated social ad plans and seamlessly turning them into easy-to-follow revenue-producing campaigns.

His agency manages over $3 million per month in paid advertising via Facebook, Instagram, and YouTube.

He was been rated as one of the top "Experts to Watch" by Forbes Magazine, has been featured on Entrepreneur.com, Business Insider, The Huffington Post, and been interviewed on various podcasts and web shows around the topic of social advertising.

Contact David at david@convertroi.com for speaking opportunities and small business consulting.

ACKNOWLEDGMENTS

I would like to acknowledge everyone who played a role in supporting me throughout this journey.

My parents, who supported me with love and support since day 1 to start my business and tackle my dreams.

Without you, I could never have reached this current level of success.

Secondly, my wife Erica who has provided patient, advice, and guidance throughout this process.

Thank you for allowing me to work hard for what I believe in through thick and thin.

Without you, I could have never made it this far. I love you.

Printed in Great Britain
by Amazon

43527355R00116